✳ Like the first quilt I ever made, ✳
this book is for my mom.

# CONTENTS

# MODERN LOG CABIN
# QUILTING

25 Simple Quilts and
Patchwork Projects

✳ Susan Beal ✳

POTTER
CRAFT

New York

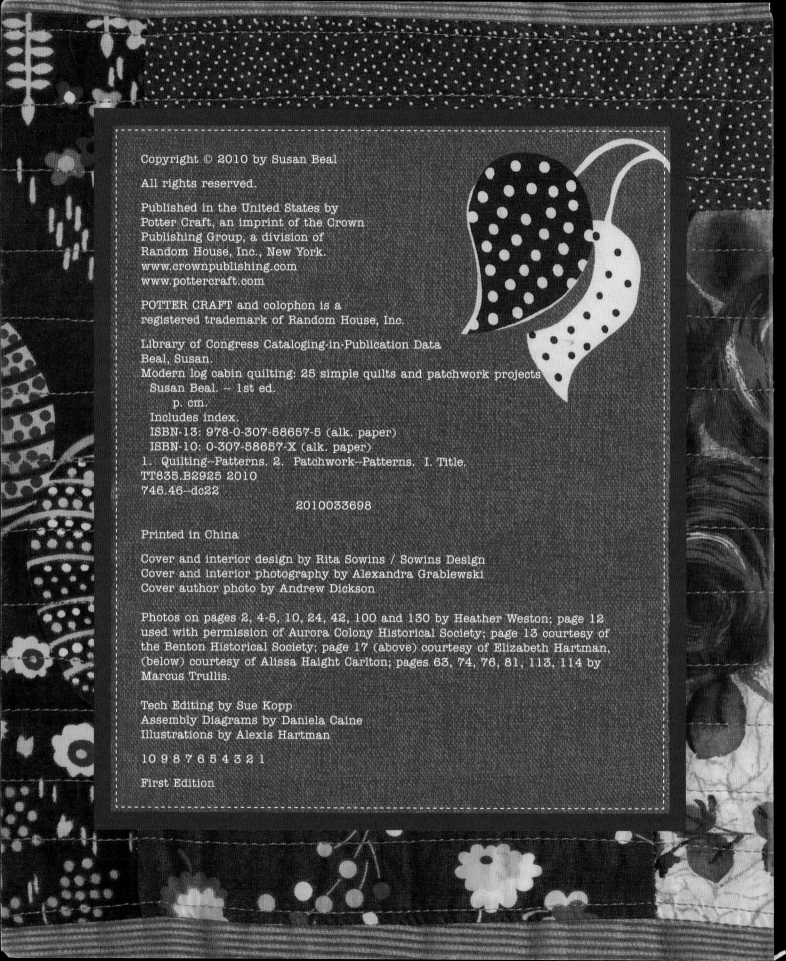

Published in the United States by
Potter Craft, an imprint of the Crown
Publishing Group, a division of
Random House, Inc., New York.
www.crownpublishing.com
www.pottercraft.com

POTTER CRAFT and colophon is a
registered trademark of Random House, Inc.

Library of Congress Cataloging-in-Publication Data
Beal, Susan.
Modern log cabin quilting: 25 simple quilts and patchwork projects
   Susan Beal. -- 1st ed.
      p. cm.
   Includes index.
   ISBN-13: 978-0-307-58657-5 (alk. paper)
   ISBN-10: 0-307-58657-X (alk. paper)
1. Quilting--Patterns. 2.  Patchwork--Patterns.  I. Title.
TT835.B2925 2010
746.46--dc22

                    2010033698

Printed in China

Cover and interior design by Rita Sowins / Sowins Design
Cover and interior photography by Alexandra Grablewski
Cover author photo by Andrew Dickson

Photos on pages 2, 4-5, 10, 24, 42, 100 and 130 by Heather Weston; page 12
used with permission of Aurora Colony Historical Society; page 13 courtesy of
the Benton Historical Society; page 17 (above) courtesy of Elizabeth Hartman,
(below) courtesy of Alissa Haight Carlton; pages 63, 74, 76, 81, 113, 114 by
Marcus Trullis.

Tech Editing by Sue Kopp
Assembly Diagrams by Daniela Caine
Illustrations by Alexis Hartman

10 9 8 7 6 5 4 3 2 1

First Edition

# ✛ FALLING IN LOVE WITH **LOG CABIN** ✛

I've always been crafty and had been sewing, making jewelry, screen printing, and teaching and writing about all kinds of crafts for years before I ever tried quilting. I was selling my handmade skirts, handbags, and jewelry at craft fairs and stores nationwide; contributing to magazines like *ReadyMade, Bust, Adorn,* and *Craft*; and had even started a craft collective, Portland Super Crafty, with my friends—but I still found quilting intimidating. I was eager to make a real quilt and had so many ideas in my head (and so much fabric in my stash!), but cutting and following a complex pattern seemed overwhelming, and I wondered if those fabrics I adored separately would really look as good stitched closely together.

Fortunately, deep into designing the 150 jewelry projects for my second book, *Bead Simple,* I hosted a craft night for some of my friends and got up the nerve to quilt for the very first time. I chose a handful of prints in blues and yellows and started cutting wide strips of fabric to try my very first log cabin block. I kept my center square large enough to spotlight the fabric design: a vintage repeating print of tiny birds in nests on a sky-blue background. On an impulse, I mixed in thinner rows of corduroy reclaimed from an old pair of pants to "frame" the patterned fabrics I liked so much . . . and then I suddenly had a finished quilt block, ready to turn into a pillow cover. I was in love! I finished a second version of what I decided to call my Recycled Cords Pillows the same night. This sweet pair of pillows still adorn my couch six years later, and they make me happy every time I see them. Since then, I've designed and sewed lots more quilts, exhibited some of them in shows, studied improvisational piecing with my quilting hero Denyse Schmidt, and even taught at Pacific Northwest College of Art in Portland—and log cabin has found its way into nearly all of my quilting endeavors.

Log cabin quilting, a simple and artful way to piece strips of patterned or plain fabric around a central square to build a geometric block, is the perfect way to get started quilting—or to bring quilting techniques into your sewing and other crafts. The log cabin block pattern is intuitive, easy to understand, and only uses straight-line stitching, so there are no tricky angles or finicky seams to navigate. The basic idea is incredibly adaptable, and your color, pattern, and arrangement choices ensure a very personal outcome.

In this book, you'll learn the general technique of piecing and quilting blocks, and then put those skills into practice by using these handmade squares to adorn or construct very modern quilts, bags, gifts, and essentials for the home. I've included ten quilts and fifteen other projects, from full-size bags to tiny camera cases, using some of my favorite log cabin styles for a streamlined, modern take on this "old-fashioned" art form.

Introduction

So what does "modern" log cabin quilting mean, anyway? Making a modern quilt doesn't mean you need to follow a minimalist or super-specific aesthetic. Instead, "modern" quilting simply seeks to impart a fun, fresh look to the craft's venerable and lovely traditions. For some sewers, it's all about fabric choice; for others, it's changing the size, shape, or scale of log cabin blocks or using improvisational piecing or lively colorwork. For me, modern log cabin quilting focuses on the aspects of quilting I love the most—making a project that is structurally simple, but meaningful and fun to craft, that conveys a message through design and embellishment choices, and is quilted simply so the design and piecing can live together happily.

This is such an exciting time for modern quilt-making, with developments including (of course) new log cabin designs, and amazing fabrics, battings, and other high-quality tools and materials much easier to find. Modern quilt guilds have sprung up worldwide, and swaps of fabric, blocks, and quilted projects (both online and local) bring the venerable quilting bee beautifully up to date. The fresh, accessible sensibility and energetic spirit that defines modern quilting feels especially apt for log cabin, which has always been a quilt pattern for the everyman and woman.

In *Modern Log Cabin Quilting*, you'll find what makes your projects uniquely modern, following the traditional rules—or not. Along with basic sewing and quilting techniques, there are plenty of ideas and instructions for personalizing your log cabin projects with printing, photo transfer, embroidery, appliqué, and other methods. I've also shared all the tips and handy shortcuts I've learned from years of quilting and making other crafts, which I hope you'll find super helpful too! I love searching for vintage and new fabric (and buttons, and embroidery floss, and felt . . .), so I included a resources guide for finding all the materials you'll need (Resources, page 156). And you can see even more ideas at the companion website modernlogcabinquilting.com. I hope you'll add some of your own pictures there—I would love to see what you make!

**Happy quilting!**
**Susan**

# ❖ HOW TO USE **THIS BOOK** ❖

Log cabin is one of the most accessible and beginner-friendly quilt-block patterns, and it's a lovely and versatile technique to mix into sewing and patchwork projects, too. You won't need many tools or materials beyond basic sewing supplies, so you can get started quickly. In Chapter 1 you'll learn everything you need to know to piece each of the five styles of log cabin used in this book, as well as how to choose the best patterns and fabrics for your project. Then, in Chapter 2, some general log cabin quilting and sewing techniques will prepare you to make every project in the Quilts, Home Decor, and Bags + Beyond chapters.

I've rated the quilt and patchwork projects by difficulty, from one to five spools of thread. It's a time-honored system—antique quilts representing months of beautiful handwork were described by the number of spools of thread each one required. You'll find the difficulty levels noted for you at the beginning of each project. Keep in mind that because log cabin blocks are made using straight lines and stitches, even the most advanced projects are totally doable!

🧵     **Perfect for brand-new sewers, very accessible**

🧵🧵     **Beginner-friendly, with some new skills involved**

🧵🧵🧵     **Uses a few intermediate techniques such as intentional block placement or making pockets**

🧵🧵🧵🧵     **More challenging for intermediate sewers**

🧵🧵🧵🧵🧵     **Most involved in skill and experience, or uses detailed embellishments**

Each project also includes a Cutting Key to show you exactly what you'll need to cut and prepare for each project, with notes indicating the fabrics I chose for reference. Use this section to select the type and amount of fabric you'll need—it's also perfect for figuring out which projects are stash-friendly! Other handy details like which techniques are used; assembly and block diagrams; finished sizes for center squares, logs, and projects; and other requirements are included at the beginning of each project, too.

A note on measurements: In the interest of streamlining the instructions and keeping our measurements as accurate as possible, the projects include dimensions in inches, feet, and yards only—log cabin's cutting and piecing is so simple that the conversions shouldn't be taxing. I hope sewists and quilters whose first numbers-language is metric find the projects and instructions as easy and accessible as we do here in the States. I am always available through my website modernlogcabinquilting.com to answer any questions you might have!

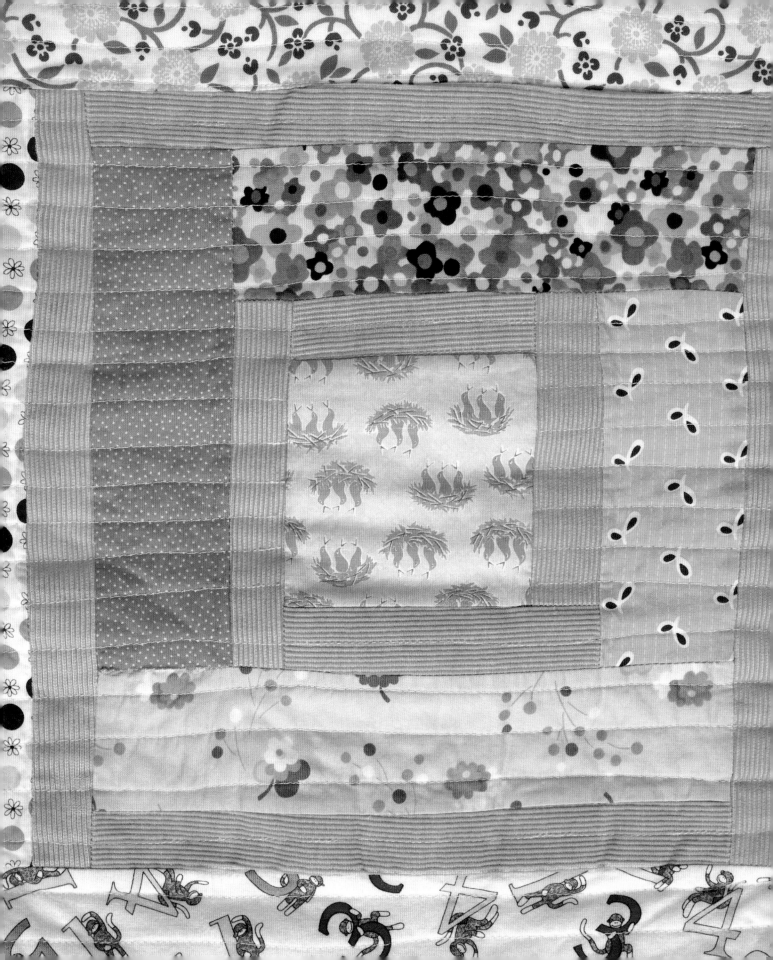

# CHAPTER 1

# BEGINNING WITH

# ❋ LOG CABIN ❋

**If you've always wanted to make a quilt**—or bring quilt-making techniques into your other crafts—log cabin is the perfect place to begin. Typically, every block in a log cabin quilt is pieced, or sewn, together using the same basic method. Strips of cloth called logs are sewn in tiers around a center square. These log cabin blocks can be made as large or small as you like—some quilts are made of just one huge block! This simplicity makes the pattern easy to cut and sew. You need only master straight lines and right angles. There's no fussing with complex math or difficult-to-align seams.

Each quilt block can be sewn as a complete design, independent of its neighbors, or the blocks may be joined together to create eye-catching patterns of light and dark values that often seem to undulate on the quilt top, the patchwork layer on the front of a quilt. Designers use the placement of light- and dark-colored logs to achieve these fascinating visual effects—a hallmark of traditional log cabin design.

Barn Raising quilt made by Emily Giesy Miller, circa 1890, from the collection of the Aurora Colony Historical Society.

## A BRIEF HISTORY

Within the structure of log cabin lie endless possibilities, depending on the arrangement of the logs around the center and the placement of blocks in the overall patchwork or quilt design. Although no one is sure *exactly* when and where log cabin originated, the pattern has been documented in quilts as early as the 1820s. In the decades that followed, the popularity of log cabin rose (particularly on Isle of Man) and the quintessentially American appeal of this pattern was soon established in the United States.

The rise of log cabin quilts was also fueled by the new availability of mass-produced textiles and a novel machine from I. M. Singer and Company in the 1850s. The sewing machine allowed women to quickly create utilitarian quilts—workhorses for everyday use—and log cabin quilts were an especially simple and efficient pattern for quilts like these. Meanwhile,

log cabin quilts followed the Oregon Trail to Oregon and California, both as precious family treasures and comforting everyday necessities. The pattern was simple enough to teach even the youngest sewers on the wagons and sturdy enough to hold up through such a long and arduous journey.

But log cabin quilting reached true popular fervor in the United States as Abraham Lincoln campaigned for the presidency, emphasizing his childhood in a log cabin on the American frontier. The quilt pattern took on a patriotic resonance as the Union split, and many historians have noted that it was a fashionable choice for fundraising for the Union cause in 1863, when handmade quilts were raffled off to support the troops. Lincoln's death in 1865 brought untold numbers of memorials and tributes—including log cabin quilts. Log cabin flourished magnificently through the remainder of the 1800s, mixed with crazy quilting

Picture Frames quilt
made in 1865, from the
Susan Cockrell collection
of the Benton County
Historical Society.

for fancy "show quilts" of silk, wool, and velvet, or in stand-alone designs like the artful Barn Raising, Straight Furrows, and Sunshine and Shadow arrangements.

Log cabin's popularity continued through the twentieth century. Its efficient, utilitarian piecing structure made it an economical choice for quilters during the Great Depression and in the 1940s, when World War II brought rationing of many civilian products. The scrap-quilting mentality of log cabin was prized by women across the country, but it found a special place among the Amish in Pennsylvania and in the rural South, including the quilters of Gee's Bend, Alabama. This community of quilters, still active today, created stunning, architectural quilts and recently became well known through a major exhibition at the Museum of Fine Arts, Houston, in 2002. One of the most notable Gee's Bend styles is Housetop, a log cabin variation on a huge scale.

Today, galleries and museums continue to show quilts as art pieces, contemporary improvisational quilters such as Denyse Schmidt create of-the-moment log cabin designs, and charming Japanese quilt and craft books have given patchwork quilting a new renaissance. Modern quilt guilds have formed all around the world, with members incorporating log cabin piecing into their designs to spotlight both vintage fabrics and new designer collections, and incorporating updated elements like "wonky" off-kilter centers and logs. The log cabin pattern is as fresh and modern today as it is traditional, and its creative applications are simply endless.

### QUILT LIKE AN EGYPTIAN

The log cabin pattern might just be more "traditional" than we think. A very similar design was found on the linen wrappings of Egyptian mummies. Many mummies were shipped to Great Britain at just the time, quilting author Jane Hall points out, that the log cabin quilting pattern coincidentally began its meteoric rise. It's unclear if Victorian-era quilters really were following a "mummy craze," but this story does show just how classic the log cabin pattern is.

## DESIGNING LOG CABIN BLOCKS

By definition, log cabin design pairs centers with concentric layers of "logs." Most traditionally, a log cabin block includes a red (sometimes yellow) center square, said to represent the hearth of the home (or lamplight), surrounded by light strips of fabric on one side and dark strips on the other. These logs show the sides of a log cabin's walls in "sunshine and shadow" and split the block into two diagonal halves of color. Basic Sunshine and Shadow blocks can be arranged throughout a quilt in a variety of patterns, depending on how the blocks are oriented and joined together. Quilters arrange their blocks to yield dazzling results, delicately balancing lights and darks to trick and lead the eye.

The dizzying array of fabrics available now have fed quilters' creativity to explore changes in center shape and sizes, color play, and other elements that transform the basic template. To get you started, I've chosen five styles of log cabin blocks for the quilts and patchwork in this book. These are my favorites, and range from traditional to very modern. All use the simplest and most straightforward of the log cabin piecing structures—perfect for beginning quilters and easy to incorporate into almost any sewing project. Use this section as a guide as you choose your fabrics and create your own designs.

**1. Sunshine and Shadow (also known as Light and Dark)**
This traditional log cabin block configuration allows quilters to create a series of high-contrast lines or shapes that seem to melt from dark to light. The block orientation and overall placement dictate the quilt pattern.

Piece the block: Use light-colored fabrics for two logs of each tier in the block. Use dark-colored fabrics for the adjacent two logs, and so on.

Used in: Sunshine and Sock Monkeys Baby Quilt (page 45), Modern Crosses Quilt (page 65), Bright Furrows Quilt (page 77), Clouds in the Sky Duvet Cover (page 83), Favorite Fabrics Bag (page 145), Red Cross Bag (page 151).

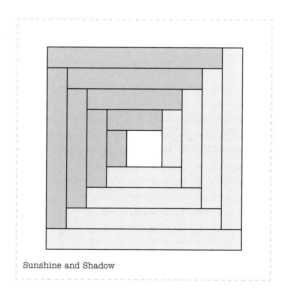

Sunshine and Shadow

## Sunshine and Shadow Assembly Diagrams

The basic Sunshine and Shadow style can create many
different quilt designs, based on block placement and
orientation.

Light and Dark

Sunshine and Shadow

Streak of Lightning

Barn Raising

Straight Furrows

Designing Log
Cabin Blocks

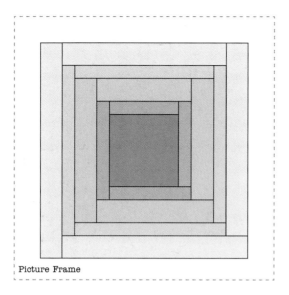

Picture Frame

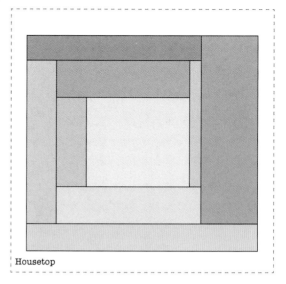

Housetop

### 2. Picture Frame (also known as Cabin in the Cotton)

The traditional name for this style is Cabin in the Cotton, but I like to call it Picture Frame because a tier of same-color fabric "frames" the blocks. This style can be used in partnership with others, such as Color Story and Random. Although I've seen this streamlined, spare arrangement used in log cabin quilts made as early as 1865 (page 13), it has a decidedly modern feel.

Piece the block: Choose which tier(s) you would like to be the frame in the block. Build the block (page 28), piecing all four logs of the frame tier from the same fabric.

Used in: Winter Woolens Quilt (page 49), T-Shirt Memory Quilt (page 59), Anniversary Quilt (page 95), Favorite Cloth Napkin and Coaster Set (page 103), Cheerful Pot Holders (page 107), Color Block Tea Towels (page 110), Polka-Dot Pincushion (page 113), Block Pocket Apron (page 117), Recycled Cords Pillow (page 124), Starry Night Pillow (page 127), Market Tote (page 141)

### 3. Housetop

Housetop, a lively, huge-scale take on log cabin, is an inventive and eye-catching style notably created by the quilters of Gee's Bend. Imagine a single log cabin block the size of a quilt top, or four blocks sewn together to form a full-size quilt, and you'll quickly get the idea. The large centers and logs lend themselves to fabrics with large-scale prints much more effectively than other log cabin styles.

Piece the block: Build the block (page 28) using as many tiers as needed for your project.

Used in: Housetop Quilt (page 53)

### 4. Color Story

An exciting and emerging style of log cabin quilting, Color Story is the term I've coined to describe the intentional use of color to create echoing and evocative patterns within a block or overall quilt, just as light and dark values would be used in a more traditional log cabin quilt. Color Story can be paired with Picture Frames for a striking arrangement.

Piece the block: Choose a color palette and find harmonious prints or solids in those color families. Cut center squares and logs as needed (page 27) and arrange each color to create the desired effect, whether symmetrically or in other reflecting or relative designs. Build each block (page 28) using as many tiers as needed for your project.

Used in: Cheerful Pot Holders (page 107), Color Story Pillow (page 121), Charming Camera Case (page 138)

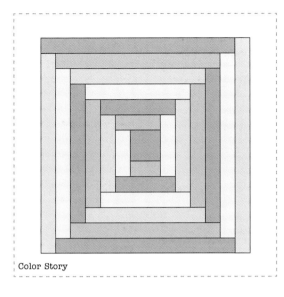

Color Story

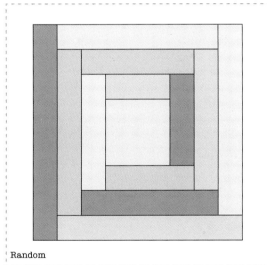

Random

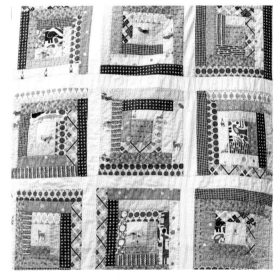

## 5. Random

Perhaps the most modern of all piecing styles, random log cabins forgo the intentional color groupings of Sunshine and Shadows, Color Story, and Picture Frame styles to create a lovely mix of fabrics without "rules." However, the log cabin piecing structure is the same, allowing any number of scraps, colors, or prints to remain orderly neighbors within their neat geometric homes.

Piece the block: Build the block (page 28) using as many different fabrics as you like.

ABOVE: Modern quilt designer and author Elizabeth Hartman's Paintbox quilts use Log Cabin to stunning effect. The exuberant but balanced Color Story, arranged in Picture Frames configuration, show the power of arranging hues artfully across a full design.

BELOW: This baby quilt by Modern Quilt Guild founder and quilt book author Alissa Haight Carlton showcases random piecing. The limited color palette of blues, browns, greens, and whites gives the blocks a stylish feel.

Used in: Vintage Linens Quilt (page 71), Recycled Cords Pillow (page 124), Drawstring Bag (page 132), Everything-in-One-Place Zip Bag (page 135), Charming Camera Case (page 138), Favorite Fabrics Bag (page 145)

## VARIATIONS EXTRAORDINAIRE: COURTHOUSE STEPS AND PINEAPPLE

Two venerable takes on log cabin, Courthouse Steps and Pineapple, are gorgeous variations on the basic log cabin piecing structure.

Courthouse Steps pairs logs of equal length on opposite sides of the center square for a streamlined piecing process and intriguingly different visual. Pineapple is a fanciful version of log cabin with carefully angled strips radiating out from square or octagonal centers! The typical light and dark contrasts take on new complexity in this dazzling setting.

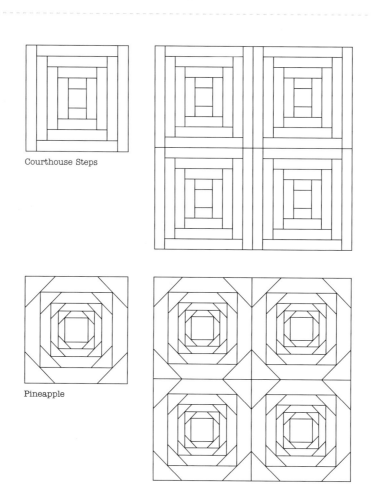

Courthouse Steps

Pineapple

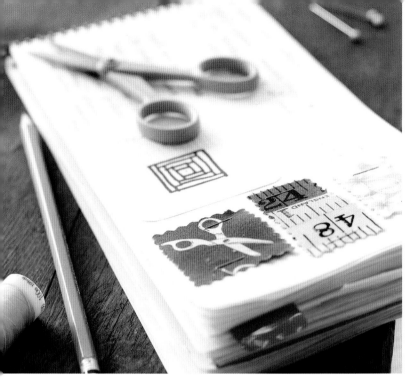

Sketchbook page for the Color Story Pillow (page 121)

**Tip:** Is your design looking too busy? Swap in solid fabrics. You can even use very-small-scale prints to mimic a solid color. That's because, at a distance, the eye organizes prints into colors. It's only up close that you might realize that what appears to be a solid color fabric is actually a tiny print!

### ✳ Planning Your Design ✳

Swatching or placing folded fabric together is my absolute favorite way to plan a log cabin design. Your two greatest allies here are natural light and a white or neutral flannel design board. This large piece of flannel, either hung on the wall or laid on your work surface, holds swatches, blocks, and **sashing** (the fabric sewn between blocks) in place without pinning. The neutral hue of the flannel lets you see whether fabrics work together harmoniously, and the sticky nap of the flannel allows you to swap fabrics and blocks as you like to achieve your favorite combinations. Look at your proposed pairings up close, then walk away and examine them from a distance. You may see things very differently from these two perspectives and get new ideas to substitute or add colors and prints.

A sketchbook or gridded paper is also a great tool. You can use colored pencils (my favorite) or markers to draw basic log cabin quilt blocks on the grid, discarding combinations you don't like, until you isolate the look you're after. My sketches also include a simple drawn quilt block, a short written description of the project (number of blocks, finished size, any embellishments, and so on), and several fabric swatches. The sketchbook can be updated as you work and is a nice visual record for long-term projects. Many quilters, including my friend and collaborator Daniela Caine, also design on their computers, which is a fantastic way to pair fabrics or colors and change your options (and dimensions) instantly.

### CHOOSING FABRIC

The success of your log cabin design depends on the fabric you choose. Quilt design is based so much on personal preference, of course, but there are some basic principles to designing with fabric.

I like to think of the fabrics that ultimately mix into a quilt or patchwork project in terms of major players supported by prints and solids. Depending on what style of log cabin you want to make, your major players may vary. In a Sunshine and Shadow quilt, for example, major players will be determined by color value—the overall lightness or darkness of a fabric. In a Picture Frames quilt, however, your major players will likely be fabrics with a special print you'd like to showcase, "framed" by neutrals or other prints. In general, when choosing combinations for your quilt blocks, aim for a mix of small, busy prints and solid-color fabrics that support a few larger-scale "impact" prints.

## ✳ Types of Fabric ✳

**Quilting cottons** are ideal for making patchwork projects and quilts (as the name suggests). These fabrics are typically light- to mid-weight woven cotton, usually about 44″ wide off the bolt. They have a crisp feel when new, often due to sizing and manufacturing, and a lovely hand after washing. Quilting cottons cut and piece nicely and hold their shape well in finished projects.

When you can, stock up on yardage of fabrics you want to use as a major player. You'll usually use about ½ yard for making your own binding, and up to two yards or so for wide or substantial sashing. If you love a fabric but don't see it as a major component in a design, a **fat quarter** (¼ yard cut to 18″ x 22″ instead of 9″ x 44″) may provide just the right amount of fabric for piecing Color Story or Random log cabin blocks.

Log cabin's relatively small piecing structure allows you to incorporate several different types of fabric into a block or project if you like. This makes log cabin an inexpensive design choice and great for using scraps or stash-busting! In general, keep in mind that it's easiest to sew together fabrics of the same weight—quilting cottons to quilting cottons, jersey to jersey—and that seams joining different types of fabric will be weaker. Also keep in mind that a project is only as durable as its weakest fabric or seam, so make choices appropriate to the intended use of your quilt or patchwork. However, with a careful eye on the tension of your stitches, and a few helpful tips, you can successfully integrate multiple fabrics into a project. Following are guidelines for including some of my favorite fabrics.

✳ **Corduroy:** Light- or medium-weight corduroy quilts nicely when cut on grain and mixes well with other fabrics. Do not piece it too narrowly; skinny strips get bulky, so cut logs 1½″ or wider.

✳ **Denim**: Use light- or medium-weight denim for larger-scale projects, or as a "batting" layer (page 135 and 151) between a pieced top and a backing fabric to add strength and shape. Denim

## FABRIC TERMS

Here are a few of the handiest terms to know when working with fabric.

The fabric's **selvage** is the finished edge on each edge of your fabric perpendicular to where it was cut off the bolt, often printed with the manufacturer's information on one side and left blank on the other. Many fabrics have a **right** (printed) and **wrong** side.

The fabric's **fold line** is its approximate halfway point when folded selvage to selvage, where it's folded on the bolt.

**Grain** refers to the directional weave of your fabric: **lengthwise grain** runs parallel to the selvage, and **crosswise grain** runs perpendicular. When you cut a woven fabric like quilting cotton **on grain**, your fabric will press and piece smoothly, lie flat, and resist stretching or shifting, all of which makes for neater and more accurate finished quilt blocks. When you cut a fabric on the **bias,** you are cutting at a 45-degree angle to the selvage, which gives your fabric stretchiness on-grain fabric doesn't have.

## ORGANIZE YOUR FABRIC STASH

Dipping into your stash can be a great way to make your projects ultra-personal—maybe the bits and pieces left over from sewing your kitchen curtains or a favorite dress are just the thing to mix into a new quilt. One log-cabin-specific trick I've learned is to keep clear gallon Ziploc® bags of extra fabric strips from past projects handy, organized by width. So I have a bag of 1" strips, a bag of 1½" strips, a bag of 2" strips, and so on. This organizational trick makes Color Story and Random piecing especially easy.

does not take precision pressing as easily as a thinner cotton but will hold a folded seam well. I recommend using a ⅜" or ½" seam allowance for medium- or heavyweight denim, and as for corduroy, make logs at least 1½" wide.

* **Flannels**: Flannels make a cozy quilt, but this fabric has a bit more stretch and shift than typical woven cottons do. In my experience, this makes them harder to machine-quilt, so I like to hand-tie projects that use this fabric.

* **Jersey**: It's a lot of fun to see old T-shirts reinterpreted in a new project, but sewing and cutting jersey material can be challenging. Make it as easy as possible by choosing jersey of the same thickness, fiber content, and weight, and be patient as you sew. Working with a knit like this is a different experience than sewing wovens. For more tips, refer to Sewing with Jersey Fabric, page 62.

## ✳ Preparing Your Fabrics ✳

Prewashing fabrics, following the manufacturer's instructions, will minimize the risk of dyes running, shrinkage, or other unwelcome changes in a finished quilt or patchwork project.

Press your fabrics before cutting into them. Set your iron to the setting appropriate to the fiber content, and press your fabric from the wrong side to remove wrinkles or creases before cutting strips. Using steam or a small spray bottle of distilled water will help take care of stubborn creases or wrinkles. Remember, wool loves a steam iron, so that's essential when pressing this type of fabric.

## THREAD AND BATTING

After fabric, the two most important components in quilting are thread and batting. Just as you're careful to choose high-quality fabric, you'll want to use good-quality materials for these as well.

I like to use Mettler or Gütermann sewing thread for piecing and machine quilting. I also use the more affordable Coats & Clark brand for projects that require a lot of thread. (I often use polyester thread, which is very durable, but cotton melds nicely and matches the strength of many quilting fabrics, too.) My go-to thread color for piecing and quilting is off-white, but you may want to match your thread to your fabric or use a vivid contrast color for quilting some projects. For hand-tying I use pearl cotton or wool yarn, which felts nicely when washed. Embroidery floss is perfect for cross-stitch, embroidery, and signing your quilts.

When choosing **batting**, the fluffy inner layer of a quilt, think about the needs of the project. Because log cabin has a strong piecing structure with many intersecting seams, my preference is for minimal quilting and tying, though free-motion or all-over patterns can be lovely too. Many battings (including the ones I recommend here) allow you to leave as much as 8" to 12" between your quilting lines or knots without affecting the batting's quality over time, giving you a remarkable amount of freedom in your designs. Generally, I use Quilters

Dream Green, a recycled-soda-bottle batting, or Quilters Dream Cotton. Both stitch easily, drape nicely, and wash beautifully. Quilters Dream also makes a polyester Puff version that is lovely to quilt and bind and even warmer than down.

Of course, you can find battings in a huge range of styles and materials, from whisper-thin to lofty, and in cotton, polyester, wool, and more. Choose the batting you prefer, and always check the packaging instructions for information on an appropriate quilting or tying pattern.

### TOOLS YOU NEED

Investing in a few good-quality tools will make a huge difference in your quilting. You don't need to buy expensive things all at once, but stock up when your local quilting store has a sale!

* **Sewing machine:** A good-quality machine doesn't have to be expensive, but make sure it can accommodate specialty feet. Always keep your machine's user's manual handy.

* **¼" sewing machine foot:** Perfect for piecing fabrics with a precise quarter-inch seam allowance.

* **Walking foot:** Makes quilting several layers together a breeze by feeding all of them through the machine at the same time.

* **Needles:** A variety of sewing-machine needles are crucial: I use quilting needles, sharps, and universals most of all. Keep **hand-sewing needles** handy, too, and curved quilting needles for hand-tying.

* **Tape measure**

* **Scissors:** You'll need **fabric scissors**, **pinking shears**, and **small scissors** for trimming thread.

* **Rotary cutter, mat, and quilting ruler:** A good **rotary cutter** and **self-healing cutting mat with marked grid lines** are crucial for cutting precisely. Have replacement blades for your cutter ready to go. I like a 24″ x 36″ mat for easy cutting. I use both a 24″ and 36″ **quilting ruler**, both with lip edges that rest neatly along the edge of the mat.

* **Seam ripper:** Handy for correcting piecing mistakes.

* **Pins and baster:** Have lots of **straight pins** on hand. I like the extra-long ones with bright, easy-to-spot heads.

  You'll use oversized or **curved safety pins** or a hand-held **quilting baster** to baste your quilt sandwich.

* **Steam iron and ironing board**

* **Design board:** Several yards of wide white flannel fabric are ideal for a design board (Planning Your Design, page 19).

* **Pattern paper:** I like the semiopaque woven pattern paper with inches marked.

* **Washable fabric marker, quilt pencil, chalk, or quilter's tape:** For marking quilt lines.

* **Soft-grip quilt clips:** To hold the bulk of a quilt in a neat roll while you quilt.

* **Bias/binding-tape maker:** Use a 1″ finished-width binding-tape maker to create custom quilt bindings.

* **Bobbin winder:** For winding extra bobbins before you dive into a project!

## CHOOSING MACHINE NEEDLES

You may need to change the needle in your sewing machine as you work. I recommend you use the following types of needles as appropriate to the projects.

**Quilting:** Ideal for most piecing and quilting projects, especially when using woven fabrics such as quilting cottons.

**Sharps (sometimes called Microtex):** For piecing and quilting vintage or new sheets or other high-thread-count fabrics.

**Universal:** Generally work well with both wovens and knits and fabrics of very different weights, from jersey to wool. You may want to use ball-point needles for piecing jersey fabrics.

# CHAPTER 2 : BASIC QUILT-MAKING

## ✳ TECHNIQUES ✳

**A lot of love and time goes into a full-sized quilt.** Fortunately, basic quilt-making techniques aren't difficult to master. You'll begin by constructing the quilt top—cutting and piecing fabric, joining blocks, and adding sashes and borders if you like. Then, you'll mark quilting lines or knotting placement and start stitching—sewing or tying the quilt top, batting, and backing (the fabric on the back side of your quilt) together. Finally, you'll bind the edges of the quilt, using premade or handmade binding. The basic techniques you'll learn in this chapter will prepare you to make the quilts in Chapter 3 and the log cabin sewing projects in Chapters 4 and 5.

There are nearly as many methods, preferences, tips, and tricks for quilt making as there are quilters, so keep in mind that there are many ways to approach this craft. I have included my favorite methods, but if you prefer another way or a different process feels more natural, enjoy your own style and your own methods!

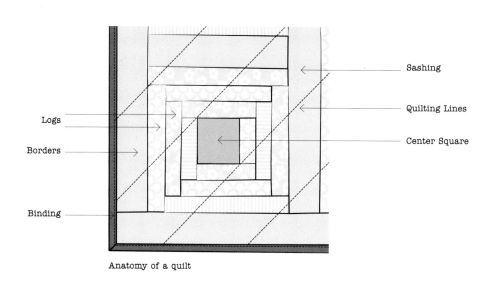

Sashing

Quilting Lines

Center Square

Logs

Borders

Binding

Anatomy of a quilt

## ANATOMY OF A QUILT

Here are the main components of a quilt, from the three layers of the quilt sandwich and the quilting that joins them to the binding that finishes your project off so neatly.

**Center squares:** Center squares are the heart of each log cabin block.

**Quilt top**: Topside of your quilt with joined blocks and optional sashing and borders.

**Logs:** You add logs around the center squares in a neat spiral to build your block outward. Four logs make each tier of the block.

**Sashing:** Strips of fabric sewn between blocks to add contrast, width, and length to a quilt top. (Not all quilts use sashing.)

**Borders**: Strips of fabric sewn to each edge of the quilt top, sometimes used to add size to a quilt top or frame the design.

**Batting and backing:** Inside your quilt is **batting**, sandwiched between the quilt top and **backing**—the pieced or plain fabric on the back of your quilt. (These aren't shown in the diagram.

**Quilting:** Quilting joins the quilt top, batting, and backing together with lines of stitching through all three layers. Knotted thread can be used to join these layers as well (page 36), in a technique called hand-tying.

**Binding:** Binding is the neatly stitched edging around the quilt that complements or contrasts with the quilt top.

# CUTTING

After choosing your fabrics and design, the first step in making a quilt is to start cutting the pieces. For log cabin quilting, you'll be cutting only strips and squares. These two shapes form every part of a log cabin design. I recommend cutting all the pieces for a project in advance so that you can efficiently reach for centers and logs when you are ready to piece your quilt blocks (page 28). Each project in this book includes a Cutting Key that shows you exactly how many pieces you'll need to cut.

For quilting, you'll use a standard ¼" seam allowance, except when otherwise noted. The measurements for all of the projects in this book include the seam allowance. Always cut any marked or perforated selvages off the bulk of the fabric so they don't show up in your quilting, and remember that your strips and centers will *each* lose ½" to the ¼" seam allowances when pieced.

Tip: If you are creating your own log cabin design, or having trouble choosing fabrics, cut just enough fabric to make one or two blocks, keeping your seam allowances in mind. Build a few sample blocks to make sure you like the dimensions and fabrics you've chosen. That way you don't have tons of beautifully cut pieces that aren't quite right for the project at hand.

To cut strips (for logs, sashing, borders, and binding), fold your pressed fabric in half, aligning it selvage to selvage, lay it out carefully on a self-healing cutting mat, trim and straighten the edge with an initial cut, and cut along the grain. Line up your quilting ruler perpendicular to the fabric (aligning your fabric with the ruler's and mat's markings) and cut it smoothly with your rotary cutter, from fold to selvage. Make sure your cut dimensions account for seam allowances; for 1"-wide strips, cut your fabric 1½" wide. If the print of your fabric is aligned differently, you may want to cut it parallel to the selvages or use another cutting method to best showcase it.

Tip: When cutting strips for long or large pieces of fabric, like sashing, borders, and binding, you may need to join shorter lengths of strips together. When you piece smaller bits of fabric together, this technique is called **scrap-piecing**.

Cut **squares** (for centers) just as you would cut strips. First, cut a strip of fabric in the appropriate width and then cut that strip into squares. This method produces a lot of centers very quickly. You'll lose ½" vertically *and* horizontally in your center square's seam allowances. For 4" x 4" squares, cut your fabric 4½" x 4½".

To cut other shapes, such as **panels** or **pockets**, follow the measurements given in the projects and use your quilt ruler and cutting mat to get the right dimensions.

Cutting mat with fabric

## PIECING AND PRESSING

Now that you have cut your fabrics for the quilt top, it's time to piece them together to create log cabin blocks. As you piece, you'll discover that great piecing cannot be separated from pressing, so have your iron ready!

### ❋ Building a Block ❋

To build a log cabin block, you join logs to the sides of a center square, rotating the block 90 degrees each time to add your new log perpendicular to the previous one. After you've built one tier of four logs, continue building tiers the same way until you've completed the block.

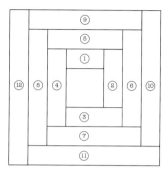

In this example above, I'm piecing clockwise—when the block grows, you'll see the new logs added in a clockwise pattern. For this first practice block, let's try a simple Picture Frames style using any three quilting cottons of your choice.

1.  To begin, cut a **3" x 3" center square** from your first fabric, a **2" x 20"** strip of your second fabric, and a **2" x 36"** strip of your third fabric. A block with these dimensions pieces together quickly and will give practice eyeing that ¼" seam allowance.

2.  Place your center square on top of the 20"-long fabric strip, right sides together, matching edges as shown. Holding them together (pinning, if desired), stitch along the shared edge, using a ¼" seam allowance. There is no need to backstitch at the beginning or the end, since the stitching line will be secured by another line of stitching.

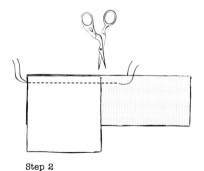

Step 2

**3.** Neatly trim the additional length of fabric from the log, set it aside, and press the back so that the seam is pressed away from the center square. In this illustration, I've pressed the back of the block and then turned it over to see the front—the first log joined to the center!

Step 3

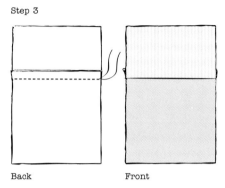

Back        Front

**4.** Position this log/center square on top of the rest of that first fabric strip, right sides together and the seam perpendicular to the strip, matching edges and ends. Holding the pieces together, stitch as before, using a ¼" seam allowance. Trim the extra log length and press. Now you've pieced the second log to the first and the center.

Step 4

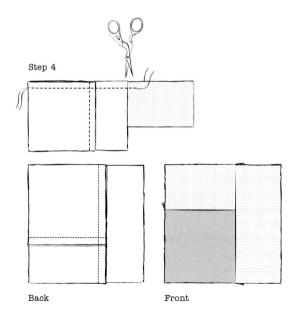

Back        Front

**5.** Piece the third log in the same manner, as shown, matching the edges and ends with the block. Hold, stitch, trim, and press. Now you have 3 logs ringing the center.

Step 5

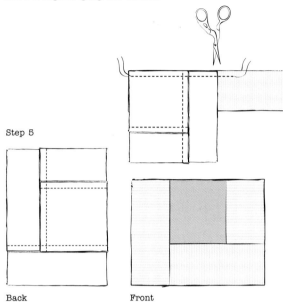

Back        Front

**6.** For the fourth log, you'll sew the strip of fabric to the open side of the center block. For the first time a corner of the center won't be at the start of your seam. Instead, begin to stitch along the shared edges of the first log, then the center, then the third log. Trim and press the block. Your first tier is done!

Step 6

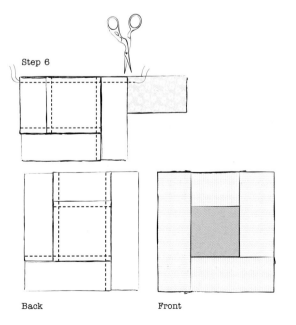

Back        Front

**7.** Piece your second tier in the same manner, using your 36" strip of fabric to form logs 5–8. You'll always begin piecing along the side with the shortest log in the previous tier—so the fifth log will join to the side of the block where the shortest (first) log is waiting.

Step 7

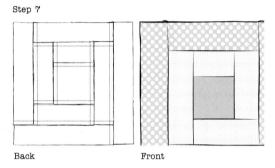

Back                     Front

Congratulations—you've finished your first log cabin block! You can add more tiers of logs, or keep it at its current size. Maybe it will become the center of a pillow front (like the Recycled Cords Pillow, page 124), or you can turn it into a simple lined bag (like the Drawstring Bag, page 132). Once you've finished this first Picture Frames block, you can experiment with Sunshine and Shadow, Color Story, and any other log cabin combinations that draw your eye.

☀ **Pressing** ☀

As you piece, you'll need to press the fabric seams. For log cabin quilting, I press my seam allowances in one direction. The geometric log cabin seams radiate out from the centers so neatly that single-direction pressing is the logical choice, in my opinion, instead of pressing the seams open. This also produces a strong, reinforced seam.

To press, set your iron to the heat setting appropriate for your fabric, and press the back of your block. The seam allowances should lie flat, the center even, and the logs neat. Flip the block over and press the front. You may want to use steam on fabrics that are resisting a dry iron. A nicely pressed block is wonderful to see!

When you're building blocks, you can press them with an iron after piecing each log, but you can often do a quick **finger-press** at your machine and keep piecing without interrupting the flow of sewing after each addition. Gently press the seam with your finger in the direction you want it to lie and then continue piecing, with the stitching anchoring the seam to that side. Generally, I finger-press my first tier of logs, and then do a thorough iron pressing of the back of the block and then the front. Then I'll add a second tier of logs, press, and

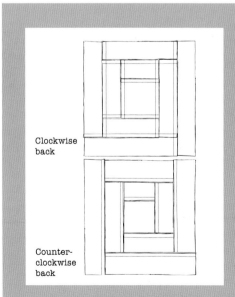

Clockwise back

Counter-clockwise back

## CLOCKWISE VS. COUNTERCLOCKWISE PIECING

Some instructions in this book will specifically call for clockwise piecing for best finished results. *In general*, the direction you piece your blocks in is up to you, and each quilter seems to have a preference.

In **clockwise piecing**, as shown in Building a Block, page 28, press your seams *away from the centers* as you go. This is more natural for the fabric and easier to stitch over. The forward motion of sewing generally works with the pressed seam, instead of against it.

In **counterclockwise piecing**, press the seams *toward the centers* as you go. The forward motion of sewing on the machine will ally with the direction of the pressing.

add a third, and so on. Use your judgment about how your fabrics and seams are behaving; for perfect precision in heavier or more temperamental fabrics, you may want to press after each seam.

### ✳ Chain-Piecing ✳

A very efficient and time-saving piecing method for a project with many similar blocks is **chain-piecing**. In this technique, multiple centers are stitched to one long strip of log fabric, cut apart, and stitched to the next long strip of log fabric. Chain-piecing is a more efficient technique than traditional piecing because it requires fewer stops and starts and uses less thread.

## CHOOSING THE RIGHT SEAM ALLOWANCE

The standard ¼" piecing allowance works well for quilting cottons and other light- and medium-weight fabrics and for closely pieced designs. However, for some fabrics, or for truly large-scale piecing, I recommend a ⅜" or ½" **piecing allowance**. For heavy fabric like denim, a ⅜" allowance lets the pressed seam lie flat a little more easily. For joining very large pieces, such as those in the Winter Woolens Quilt (page 49), a ½" allowance provides much-needed support. A ½" seam allowance is also ideal when piecing knits, such as T-shirt jersey material, to accommodate the stretch and the tendency of the edges to roll. As always, the width you lose in your seams will factor into your final measurements, so plan for the seam allowance when cutting (page 27).

1. First, put a center square on a long log strip, right sides together. Stitch the pieces together just as you would in regular piecing. Then, when you're near the end of the seam, place another center, and sew. You can keep adding more center squares until you have the number you need, or the strip runs out.

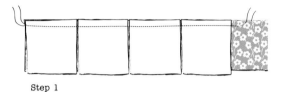

Step 1

2. Using a rotary cutter and ruler, carefully cut the joined pieces apart between the blocks and press the seams in the appropriate direction. Set up your second log strip, and place a joined center/log piece over it, right sides together. Stitch as before, adding joined center/log pieces the same way.

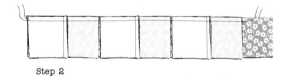

Step 2

3. Continue in the same manner to build the third and fourth logs onto your blocks. When you reach the end of the first tier of logs, press all seams well. Your block will look just like one that was individually pieced.

4. Continue chain-piecing additional tiers to the block as necessary for your log cabin pattern. The piecing will become more challenging as the seams (and logs) get longer, but gently hold them in place and slow or stop your sewing if necessary to align the seams neatly. If chain-piecing large tiers becomes too unwieldy for you, simply sew the remaining logs following the Building a Block strategy, page 28.

## JOINING BLOCKS

After you've pieced your blocks and pressed them well, square them up (neaten the sides) with a rotary cutter. The blocks may be slightly misshapen due to stretching while sewing, or have small seam allowance discrepancies, but the goal is straight edges and 90-degree corners. Then arrange and rearrange your blocks to your heart's content on the white flannel design board. If you are using sashing or borders and haven't made your final fabric selection yet, place a few completed blocks on your fabric options to help you decide. When you're happy with your design and placement, take a digital photo for a construction guide so you can remember your placement! It's time to join all those blocks into a quilt top. There are several ways to do this, depending on your design.

### ✳ Row Joining ✳

The simplest method of joining blocks is **two- and four-way joining**. To use this method, simply line up two blocks, matching edges and seams with right sides facing, and stitch them together with a ¼″ seam allowance. Press them on the back and the front. I generally don't use pins to sew the length of a single block, but you may find it helpful.

Joined pairs of blocks can be sewn into larger squares (as in the Modern Crosses Quilt, page 65). Simply align the pairs along a long unfinished side, right sides together, matching edges and seams. Pin the blocks where the seams meet to prevent the blocks from shifting during sewing. Stitch the pairs together with a ¼″ seam allowance.

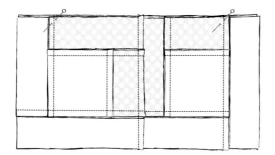

### ✳ Column Joining ✳

This method is useful for joining long columns of blocks in a larger quilt design. I like to work off a white flannel design board, starting on the left side and moving to the right, joining blocks vertically.

Step 1

1. Stack the blocks: Stack the blocks from the left-hand column, with the uppermost one on top and the lowest one on the bottom, oriented the same way. (If you want a guide other than the photo you took, I suggest putting a single straight pin in Block 1, the top block of the stack, so you don't get disoriented.)

2. Stitch the blocks: Stitch the bottom edge of Block 1 to the top edge of Block 2, right sides together, as described in the two-way joining directions. Now sew the bottom edge of Block 2 to the top edge of Block 3, and continue until your first column is joined.

3. Press the column: Press the back of the column and then the front, and replace it on the flannel.

4. Repeat steps 1–3, moving across the quilt top, to complete the assembly of each vertical column.

Column 1    Column 2

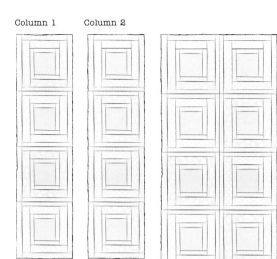

Step 4                    Step 5

5. Join the columns: Carefully pin the long right-hand edge of Column 1 (the leftmost column) to the long left edge of Column 2, right sides together, and matching seams and edges. Stitch using a ¼″ seam allowance, and press the back and front. Continue to join your remaining vertical columns the same way until you have finished your quilt top.

### ✳ Column Sashing ✳

This method is quite similar to column joining, but instead of sewing blocks together directly, sashing is sewn between each block. Sashing may be used between rows of blocks, between columns, or both!

1. Prepare sashing: You can measure your blocks and cut sashing to that length to join single blocks, or simply trim a longer strip as you join. To join columns of blocks, cut lengths of sashing slightly longer than the length of the quilt top.

2. Stack the blocks: Stack the blocks into columns as described for the column joining method, page 32.

3. Join sashing between rows: Stitch the bottom edge of Block 1 to the top edge of a length of sashing, matching ends, and trim the excess sashing away. Stitch the bottom edge of the sashing to the top edge of Block 2. Stitch the bottom edge of Block 2 to the top edge of the next length of sashing, trimming it neatly. Con-

tinue in this manner until you reach the end of the first column. Press the back of the column, pressing the sashing seam allowances toward the blocks, and then press the front.

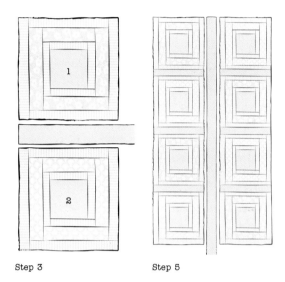

Step 3                    Step 5

4. Repeat step 3 to assemble each vertical column.

5. Join sashing between columns: Pin the long right-hand edge of Column 1 to the long edge of a length of sashing, right sides together, and stitch using a ¼″ seam allowance. Pin and stitch the long left edge of Column 2 to the unfinished long edge of the sashing, right sides together. Press the back with the sashing seam allowances toward the blocks.

6. Repeat step 5 to join the remaining columns and sashing to the quilt top.

Step 6

### ✷ Adding Borders ✷

Adding borders of fabric all around your quilt top like a final tier of logs can create a framing effect, add width and length, and ensure even edges for binding. If you'd like to add a border to your quilt, measure each side of the quilt top, cut fabric pieces to the appropriate length and width (deciding how much you'd like to add to the quilt's dimensions, and keeping seam allowances in mind), and pin them all along the edge of the quilt, one at a time. Stitch the first border to the quilt top using a ¼″ seam allowance, just as you would with sashing or blocks, and press the back and front well. Continue around the quilt top as desired. I usually like to begin with a long border strip and cut it to size in the course of piecing, and add my borders like logs on a larger scale, as you can see in the quilt diagrams for each project that uses them.

## QUILT ASSEMBLY

Now that you've completed your quilt top, it's time to plan and mark your quilting lines or knotting placement and then quilt the three layers of the quilt together. For most of the quilts and patchwork projects in this book, I focus only on basic machine-quilting, although you'll find hand-tying techniques used in the Sunshine and Sock Monkeys Baby Quilt (page 45) and Winter Woolens Quilt (page 49) to show you how simple knots can be effectively used in log cabin quilts. As a final step, you'll bind the edges of the quilt and sign your new masterpiece!

### ✷ Marking the Quilt Lines ✷

Lay out the quilt top flat and smooth on a white flannel design board, a large cutting table, or the floor. Review your design and determine what type of quilting you'd like to use. Do you want to highlight the piecing structure or minimize it? Are the pieced seams few and far between or are there many seams close together? Choose from the quilting options in the sidebar Select a Quilting Pattern (page 35), or create a quilting design of your own. Remember that straight, simple quilt lines are best for beginning quilters and will not distract from the log cabin design. I include my suggested quilting patterns for each quilt or patchwork project in this book.

After you have chosen the type of quilting lines for your project, you may want to mark them on the quilt top. I like to use a water-soluble fabric marker and a quilting ruler to draw the quilting lines. If you are making a tied or knotted project, mark dots or Xs where you'll tie knots. Knots can follow the pieced design or be relatively random. *Always* test your marker on a scrap of fabric to make sure the lines disappear with water. If you prefer, you can try using chalk, a quilting pencil, or quilter's tape.

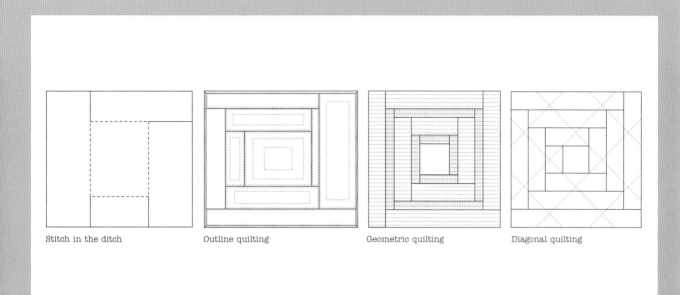

Stitch in the ditch          Outline quilting          Geometric quilting          Diagonal quilting

## SELECT A QUILTING PATTERN

I like to use simple, minimal quilting techniques on my log cabin quilts and projects, so all of the machine-quilting techniques I suggest use straight stitches and a walking foot.

**Stitch in the ditch**: One of the simplest ways to quilt a pieced design is stitch in the ditch—that is, to stitch along the existing piecing seams, following them exactly. This method highlights the areas you stitch around (like the centers of the Charming Camera Case, page 138) and doesn't visually compete with your piecing.

**Outline quilting:** Outline quilting is very similar to stitch in the ditch, but offset a certain distance, like ¼" or ½", to follow your piecing lines without actually touching them. I used this method, along with **echo quilting** (which repeats the same shapes a certain distance from the outline quilting), in the Housetop Quilt (page 53).

**Geometric quilting:** Uses straight or wonky lines, shapes, and angles to quilt over your log cabin piecing for a nice, geometric effect. In this book, I've used a variety of geometric quilting lines—like horizontal lines (Color Story Pillow, page 121) and a squared-off spiral (Recycled Cords Pillow, page 124).

**Diagonal quilting:** A neat series of diagonal lines across your quilt. These quilt lines can run in one direction, as on the Vintage Linens Quilt (page 71), or in two directions, as on the Cheerful Pot Holders (page 107).

Quilt Assembly

Tip: Don't let this step trip you up. If you are unsure of which quilting pattern to choose, you'll have plenty of time to make changes before committing to the actual quilting. Lay out a general plan, then take a break from the project. Return in a few hours to take a fresh look.

## ❋ Quilting ❋

With your quilting lines marked, you'll next need to sandwich all the layers of the quilt together.

1. First, lay out your pressed backing fabric, right side down. (This can be a single sheet, a pieced design, or whatever you choose for the underside of your finished quilt.) Smooth it out and, if necessary, tape the edges to your work surface. The backing should measure about 4″ wider and longer than your finished quilt top.

2. Next, lay your batting out over the backing, smoothing it down so there are no wrinkles or folds. (You can also briefly put batting into a low-heat dryer to remove any folds.)

3. Finally, put your pressed, marked quilt top over the batting, right side up, and center it evenly on the backing and batting.

4. Baste the layers together using safety pins or a tool called a quilt baster to join all 3 layers, working from the center of the quilt outward, and placing your pins or the basting tabs 6″ apart—closer if you'd like. You are ready to actually quilt!

5. If you are beginning to quilt in the center of your design (see Step 6), start by setting your stitch length to 0 and stitching in place for several stitches, or just backstitch the first few stitches, to begin your quilting line more securely. Use a normal stitch length to begin machine quilting, adjusting the length longer if need be as you stitch forward. Use perfect-match thread colors for the most subtle effect, off-white or neutral thread for a calm and orderly feel, or a bright or contrast color to bring energy to your quilting.

6. Begin quilting in the center sections, following your quilting lines from the middle outward. To contain the bulk of a full-sized quilt, you can roll it up on one side and hold it in place with a few soft-grip quilt clips. The rolled section fits neatly into the crook of your sewing machine, while the unrolled side can extend outward. Resting the bulk of the quilt's weight on a chair or a sturdy shelf or table just to the left of your sewing table will make the sewing easier.

7. Go slowly as you turn corners or change direction. Check the quilt back often to make sure it's smooth.

## TYING

Log cabin is a perfect candidate for hand-tying because of the strong piecing structure of the blocks. Early quilts used sturdy **foundation piecing** methods, in which the center square lay on a piece of fabric and the logs were joined to both layers. Quilters then used strategically placed knots to secure the layers of the quilt together. Sewing quilting lines by hand on such a quilt would have been nearly impossible.

In deference to tradition, I like to incorporate hand-ties into my log cabin designs whenever possible to secure the layers of my quilts and patchwork. Hand-tying is a great option when using fabrics like wool or flannel, which can be harder to machine-quilt, or when you don't want to clutter a project with quilting lines. I use two basic methods of tying quilts in this book. Both are very simple to do. Hand-tying usually leaves visible tails, which can look nice on a quilt top. Machine-tying often looks more subtle, like tufts.

To **hand-tie** a quilt:

1. Thread a curved quilting needle with pearl cotton, wool yarn, or the thread of your choice, and pierce all 3 layers of the quilt, from front to back, where you want the first knot. Bring the needle back through the fabric about ½″ from the entry point, pulling your thread all the way through and leaving about a 4″ tail.

**2.** Take a second stitch the same way, in about the same spot, and pull it taut.

**3.** Trim each end of the working thread to about 4″ and make a square knot. To make this knot, think of your 2 working thread ends as A (darker in this illustration) and B (lighter). Start with a simple tie, so A crosses over and to the left of B. Bring the ends to cross, A over B, carefully making a single tie again, so A is now to the right and B to the left, and tighten it to secure. Think of it as right over left and left over right, if that's simpler for you.

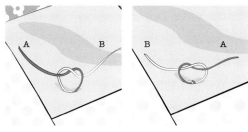

Step 3

**4.** Give the thread tails a sharp tug to make sure the knot is secure. This step is important! It's easy to accidentally tie the tails in the opposite order, making a "granny knot" that unties fairly easily. Cut off the 2 thread ends to a neat ½″–1″ long.

To **machine-tie** a quilt:

**1.** Set your sewing machine to a zigzag stitch and adjust the length and width of the stitch to 0. Place your needle over the first place you want to tie, and make several stitches in place.

**2.** While sewing, adjust your width upward to a wide setting and stitch at that setting for 5–10 seconds, or 10 or so stitches, and then adjust the width right back down to 0 for the last few stitches.

You can move your quilt around to machine-tie multiple spots without cutting the threads in between, if you like. I "tie" about ten spots before stopping, cutting and trimming my threads, and moving to a different section of the quilt. To dress up the look of the machine ties, sew buttons over the stitches, as shown in the Modern Crosses Quilt (page 65).

### ✳ Binding the Quilt ✳

Now that your quilt sandwich is machine-quilted (or tied), you're ready to prepare it for binding!

**1.** Pin around the perimeter of the quilt top, catching all 3 layers, and press if necessary.

**2.** Machine-stitch around the perimeter ¼″ from the edge of your quilt top, using a long basting stitch. (You can also do this step after squaring up.)

**3.** Then square up the quilt top, placing your quilting ruler along the quilt top's edge, aligning it with seams, and the cutting mat under the section you are working on. Use your rotary cutter to trim away excess batting and backing, making your edges neat and straight. This is a very liberating feeling—your quilt is shedding its shaggy overhang to become neat and beautiful.

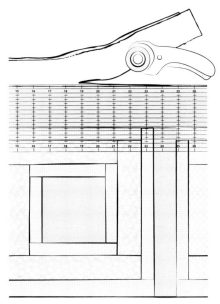

Step 3

Finally, it's time to bind your quilt! You can use purchased bias or binding tape, or make your own binding with fabrics that match, contrast, or complement your quilt design. I love making my own binding and highly recommend that route if you're up for it.

Quilt Assembly

## MAKING YOUR OWN BINDING TAPE

I prefer to use a binding-tape maker to make the binding for my projects. This tool folds strips of fabric into perfect halves and is fast and easy to use. Refer to the package instructions to determine the width to cut your strips. Then measure the perimeter of your quilt and add about 12" inches to determine the length you'll need for your project. You may need to piece multiple strips to achieve the total length needed—here's how to get started with that.

### To piece a length of binding:

1. Cut strips of fabric twice as wide as your finished binding will be. For 1" binding, I cut 2"-wide strips. (If using a binding-tape maker to fold your binding, refer to the specs provided; a few call for a slightly narrower cut, like 1⅞" to yield 1" tape.) For projects with straight edges, there is no need to cut the fabric on the bias. Cutting straight on the grain, just as you would for logs or sashing, is just fine and a lot more economical than cutting fabric at a 45-degree angle.

2. Place 2 strips of fabric perpendicular, with right sides together, as shown. Pin the strips at an angle. Stitch a diagonal line to join the strips and trim away the excess fabric, leaving a ¼" seam allowance.

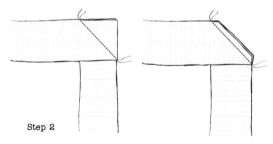

Step 2

3. Now press the seam open, and continue to join as many strips of fabric needed for your project. Once you have sewn the strips of binding together to obtain the length you need, you can fold the strips into binding.

Step 3

Tip: For a patchwork or pieced binding with many seams, you can piece your fabric strips together with a straight seam instead of an angled one. That way you have a neat, straight line, especially between high-contrast strips of fabric.

### To make the binding:

1. Cut one end of your strip at a 45-degree angle and use a straight pin to coax it through the binding-tape maker.

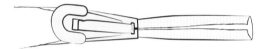

Step 1

2. Pull the fabric strip through the binding-tape maker, using an iron to press it neat and flat, with the raw edges to the middle, as you go. Every foot or two, I pause to press the 2 halves of the new tape together, creating a nice, sharp crease in the center and hiding the raw edges deep within the tape's fold.

3. As your binding tape lengthens, roll it onto an index card or empty toilet-paper roll and store it in a large plastic bag so it doesn't tangle. When the seams reach the binding-tape maker, you may need to carefully ease them through. Then press them the same way as the rest of the fabric, folding the two halves of the binding together.

4. Continue guiding, pressing, and folding your strip until you reach the end.

## ATTACHING THE BINDING

I use a simple once-around machine binding method to add binding to my quilts or other patchwork projects.

1. To machine-bind, first trim the end of your binding tape neat and straight and pin your binding along one edge of the quilt, starting about 12" from one corner. I usually start at the bottom edge, where the seam won't be as noticeable. Arrange your binding so it hugs and encloses the raw edge of your quilt sandwich, folded neatly around both sides, and is evenly distributed on the front and back of the quilt. Pin it every 3"–4" or so on that first edge.

2. Now, starting about 6" in from the end of the binding, stitch the binding down very close to its folded edge, stopping when you get to ¼" from the corner. Backstitch to hold the stitching in place. If your stitching isn't even in places, you can always do a quick seam-ripping and repinning to resew any troubled sections. This method becomes easier with practice.

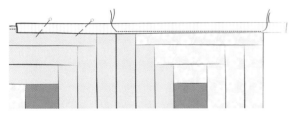

Step 2

3. Press your binding at the corner, making a neat diagonal, and fold it back over the unfinished edge, catching the end of the first seam you sewed. Pin the binding in place down the second side of the quilt.

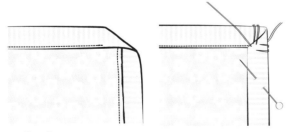

Step 3

**NOTE:** I like to baste my corners down using hand stitches to prepare them for machine-sewing. It takes an extra minute, but basting the corners instead of pinning makes it much easier to insure that the angle is perfect and that nothing shifts when a pin is pulled out. Use a contrast thread color and make big stitches, no knotting required—it will be that much easier to seam-rip or snip out when the binding has been attached.

4. Stitch from that neatly pressed corner down the length of the quilt, backstitching to hold the seam and stopping ¼" from the edge of the next corner.

Step 4

5. Continue pressing, basting, and sewing until you have stitched all 4 corners and are nearing the raw end of the binding. Stitch until about 6" before meeting the other end and stop.

6. Carefully measure ½" beyond where you started sewing the binding. Cut your working binding's end to that point. It will overlap your first edge by that crucial ½".

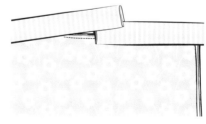

Step 6

7. Unfold both ends of the binding and pin them together, raw ends aligned and right sides together. Stitch with an exact ¼" seam allowance to join the edges together.

**8.** Press the seam allowance open, press the tape's folds back into place, and pin the binding around the edge of the quilt. It should fit snugly. If the binding is too loose or too tight, open the joining seam and adjust the seam allowance or stitch a new length of binding between the ends of the strip and resew for a perfect, snug fit.

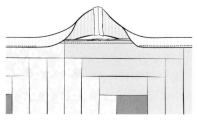

Step 8

**9.** Sew those last triumphant inches of binding, backstitching at the ends of your stitching. You have bound your quilt!

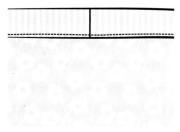

Step 9

## SPECIAL SEWING TECHNIQUES

### ✳ Appliqué ✳

Add a simple log cabin block or another decorative piece to a larger surface using this method. Just press ¼" under to the wrong side along all 4 edges of your block, clipping corners if necessary, and pin it in place on the foundation surface. Stitch all around the perimeter, backstitching at the end of the stitching to hold it in place.

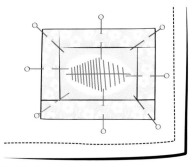

Appliqué

### ✳ Button Embellishment ✳

Add new or vintage buttons to your patchwork projects for a bit of sparkle! You can sew them onto a block before you assemble, baste, and quilt (as in the photo-transfer and printed squares on the Anniversary Quilt, page 95), or cover machine-ties or hand-ties with them as an extra embellishment (like the Modern Crosses Quilt, page 65). They can also be part of a closure (as for the Charming Camera Case, page 138 and Red Cross Bag, page 151) or just decoration for any part of a project you'd like to highlight.

Hand-stitch your buttons down very securely and make sure that they are washable, if you plan to wash your patchwork. And be very cautious about adding them to a project for a small child. The Modern Crosses Quilt will be ready for my daughter, Pearl, when she's old enough not to put those colorful, tempting buttons in her mouth!

### ✳ Double-Fold Hem ✳

This is a simple and versatile sewing technique you can use for everything from pockets to pillow backs. Simply fold the raw edge of your fabric to the wrong side and press. Then fold it once again, press, and pin it all along the fold. Stitch along the folded edge with a straight or zigzag stitch to finish the hem.

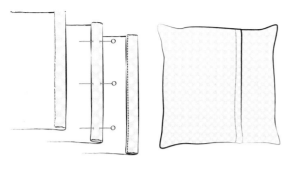

Double-fold hem                    Envelope pillow back

## ✳ Envelope Pillow Back ✳

This is an easy way to make a back for your quilt block so it fits right over a pillow form.

1.  Cut 2 pieces of fabric, each the height and over ²⁄₃ the width of the pieced pillow front. Make a double-fold hem on one side of each piece of fabric.

2.  Pin one back piece to the pillow front, right sides together, with the hem to the center. Stitch around the 3 unfinished sides.

3.  Pin the second hemmed envelope back over that first, with the hem to the center as shown, and stitch around the 3 unfinished sides, backstitching at the beginning and end to hold the seam.

4.  Trim any excess batting and fabric from the pillow front and back, clip the corners if necessary, and turn the pillow cover right side out.

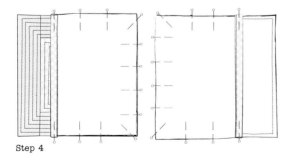

Step 4

## ✳ Patch Pocket ✳

To make and attach a basic patch pocket with reinforced corners (which is included in all the bag projects in Chapter 5):

1.  Cut a rectangle of fabric. Make a double-fold hem along the edge that will become the top. Then press the remaining 3 edges ¼" to the wrong side, clipping the corners if necessary, and pin the pocket in place on the lining or other foundation material.

2.  To sew a triangular reinforced corner at the top edge of the pocket for reinforcement, start sewing ¼" below the double-fold hem on one side edge. Stitch up at an angle to the top edge of the pocket, ½" in from the side, back-stitching at the start of the line of stitching.

3.  Rotate your project and sew until you reach the top corner of the pocket. Then rotate your project again and continue sewing around the perimeter of the pocket, down, across, and then up, until you reach the opposite top corner.

4.  Rotate your pocket and sew ½" toward the center and stop. Rotate one last time to angle down and stitch toward the edge, ¼" below the double-fold hem as for the first corner. Backstitch to hold the stitching.

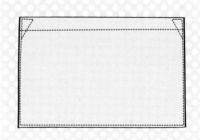

Step 4

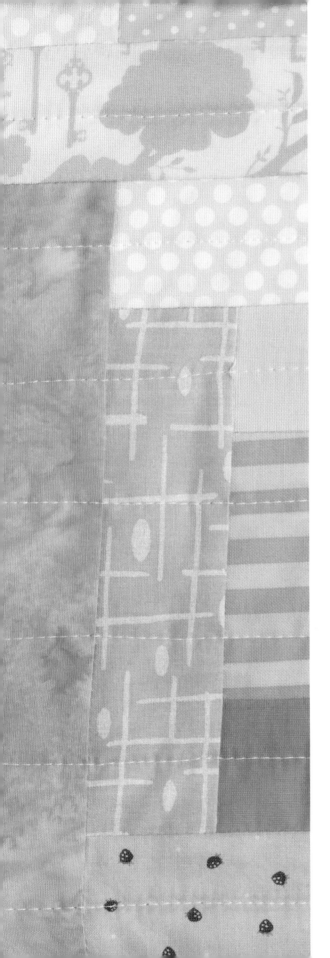

# CHAPTER 3

# ✣ QUILTS ✣

# SUNSHINE AND SOCK MONKEYS
# BABY QUILT

**Difficulty:** 🧵🧵🧵

**Type of block:** Sunshine and Shadow

**Techniques used:** spotlighting centers (page 28), column sashing (page 33), adding borders (page 34), hand-tying (page 36), binding (page 38)

This pretty baby quilt mixes in a dozen prints for a light-hearted traditional Sunshine and Shadow style. I used a super-soft flannel covered with sock monkeys for the centers, sashing, and back of the quilt and kept my color palette to sunny yellows, but any color and fabric combinations you like would work. Just make sure that the finished quilt is soft and cozy and that new parents can throw it right into the washer and dryer!

**Finished centers:** 4" x 4"

**Finished logs:** 1½" wide

**Finished block:** 9" x 9"

**Number of blocks:** 9

**Binding:** about 170" (5 yards) of 1" binding, handmade or purchased

**Finished quilt:** 40" x 40" (baby/crib)

**You'll need:**

* 2¼ yards patterned fabric (A), for center squares, sashing, and backing
* ⅛ yard *each* of 6 light-colored and 6 dark-colored fabrics (Cutting Key, Logs)
* Batting, at least 45" x 45" (I used Hobbs Heirloom Cotton batting, which can be quilted or tied up to 4" apart)
* ¼ yard fabric for binding (B), if making your own, and 1" binding-tape maker
* Pearl cotton in coordinating color and needle threader (optional)
* Thread (I used yellow for piecing and brown for binding)
* 4½" x 4½" piece of pattern paper, for spotlighting centers

| Cutting Key | A | Assorted (Light) | Assorted (Dark) |
|---|---|---|---|
| **Center Squares** | | | |
| 4½" x 4½" | 9 | - | - |
| **Logs** | | | |
| 2" x 36" | - | 6 | |
| 2" x 50" (pieced if necessary) | | | 6 |
| **Sashing and Borders** | | | |
| 3" x 44" | 8 | - | - |
| **Backing** | | | |
| 44" x 44" | 1 | - | - |
| **To make your own 1" binding:** | | | |
| Cut and join 170" of 2" wide strips (¼ yard total fabric; I used a brown polka-dot print [B]). | | | |

## Cutting

1. Choose a fun patterned fabric for your centers, sashing, borders, and backing, and find 12 other prints in a similar color palette—6 in light shades and 6 in dark. My main fabric was a yellow flannel printed with sock monkeys, and I used a dozen other yellow prints to go with it.

2. Using the Cutting Key, cut and press the fabric for the quilt. Use the pattern paper and the spot-lighting centers technique to cut out the 9 center squares. Divide the logs into 2 groups, light and dark. (I kept mine organized in two large Ziploc® bags.)

## Building the Blocks

3. Build the first block. Use one light-colored fabric for logs 1 and 2 and one dark-colored fabric for logs 3 and 4. Piece and press the first tier of the block according to the Block Assembly Diagram.

   Piece and press the second tier of logs in the same manner, using a different light-colored fabric for logs 5 and 6 and a different dark-colored fabric for logs 7 and 8. This is your first completed block.

4. Continue building 8 more blocks in the same manner, using each of your fabrics in both the first and second tiers in various blocks throughout the quilt, if possible.

**NOTE:** I used each log fabric in exactly 3 different blocks, mixing the fabrics among the first and second tiers of the blocks. No pair of fabrics appears in exactly the same combination.

**Assembly Diagrams**

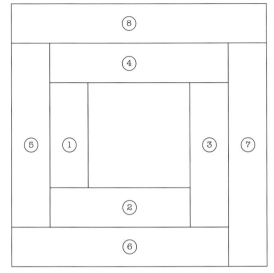

Block Assembly Diagram

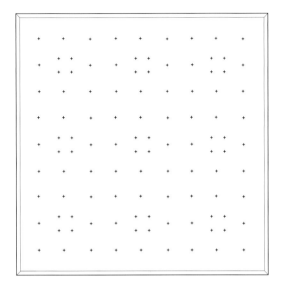

Back

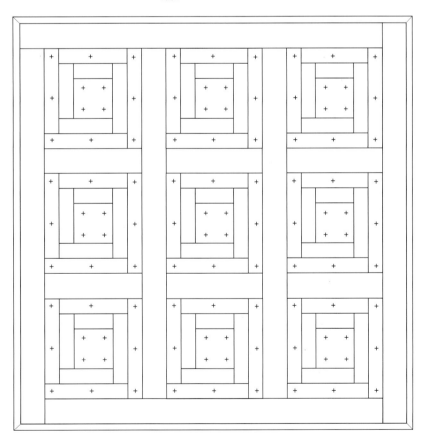

Front

+ Hand-tied knots

Sunshine and Sock
Monkeys Baby Quilt

## Assembling the Quilt

5.  When you've completed all 9 blocks, press them neatly, and arrange them on the design board in 3 rows of 3 blocks each, moving the blocks around to determine your favorite layout.

6.  Using the column sashing technique on page 33, join the first, second, and third blocks of the first column together. Press. Now join the blocks of the second and third columns, pressing each one when you complete it.

7.  Now join your first and second columns with vertical sashing, and repeat to join your second and third columns. Press.

8.  Using the adding borders technique on page 34, add the border strips to each side of the joined blocks to complete the quilt top, piecing if necessary. Press.

## Finishing the Quilt

9.  Press the quilt top. You're ready to mark your quilt top for hand-tying. Mark the knot placement according to the Front Quilt Assembly Diagram.

10. Make a quilt sandwich with your backing, batting, and quilt top, and baste them together, making sure that the layers are smooth and even. You are ready to tie!

11. Hand-tie your quilt with the pearl cotton. I tied my knots to the front, leaving 1″ tails.

12. Square up the quilt sandwich. Baste around the perimeter edges using a scant ⅛″ seam allowance.

13. Make your own binding (page 38). If using premade binding, join the pieces together as necessary. Bind the quilt to complete it.

### MAKING IT PERSONAL

This would be a wonderful quilting-bee gift for a new family; each friend could choose one-eighth yard of a printed fabric in the color range and bring it to a get-together to cut strips and centers, and bring home a set to make one block. Then one or two quilters could team up to sash, tie, and bind the quilt.

Encourage participants to choose patterned fabrics with inviting elements that babies love, like animals or familiar shapes and colors. My daughter adored the monkeys and elephants I mixed into this design and was excited to point to each one and name it.

# WINTER WOOLENS **QUILT**

**Difficulty:** 🧵🧵🧵🧵🧵

**Type of block:** Picture Frame

**Techniques used:** row joining (page 32), column sashing (page 33), hand-tying (page 36), topstitching (page 52)

My favorite place in the world is Mount Hood here in Oregon. It's beautiful all year round, but incredible in the winter—the perfect time of year to stay in a Forest Service cabin on the mountain or visit magnificent Timberline Lodge. Timberline's 1930s architecture and charming rustic decor inspired me to design this quilt. I turned to another Oregon treasure, Pendleton Woolen Mills, for the wool fabric and yarn.

**Finished center:** 22″ x 15″

**Finished logs:** 5″ wide

**Finished block:** 32″ x 25″

**Number of blocks:** 6

**Finished quilt:** 92″ x 84″ (queen)

## You'll need:

* 2 yards patterned wool fabric, at least 45″ wide (A)
* 1¼ yards plaid wool fabric, 72″ wide (or equivalent) (B)
* 1¼ yards patterned wool fabric, at least 96″ wide (or 2¾ yards of 45″-wide wool fabric) (C)
* Blanket or other backing fabric, at least 96″ x 88″
* Pencil or chopstick
* Curved needle and wool yarn for tying
* Thread (I used tan thread for piecing, topstitching, and joining)

**NOTES:**

* To support the size and scale of this quilt's center, logs, and sashing, piece the quilt top using a ½″ seam allowance. For a lighter-weight version of this design, use cotton flannel instead of wool fabric. Three flannel sheets would yield plenty of yardage for this design.

## Assembly Diagrams

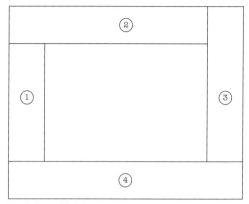

Block Assembly Diagram

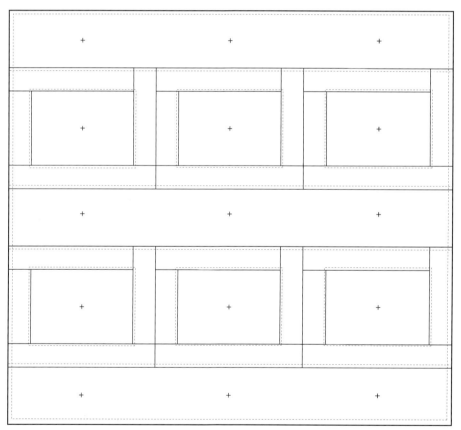

Front

+ Hand-tied knots

| Cutting Key | A | B | C |
|---|---|---|---|
| **Center Squares** | | | |
| 22½" x 15½" | 6 | - | - |
| **Logs** | | | |
| 5½" x 72" total, (B) | - | 8 | - |
| **Sashing** | | | |
| 12½" x 96" (pieced if necessary) | - | - | 3 |
| **Backing** | | | |
| 96" x 88" | | | |

**NOTE:** I used 72" wide fabric for my logs, but you can piece them from other widths. 5½" x 72" needed for the project.

Tip: I used very wide fabric for the sashing and backing in this quilt, but you can join these elements from narrower fabrics.

## Cutting

1. Using the Block Assembly Diagram as a guide, choose 3 wool fabrics, patterned or solid, that work well together for this large-scale project. Because the centers and sashing are generously sized, a large or engaging fabric pattern is ideal. I also chose a medium-scale plaid for my logs.

2. Using the Cutting Key, cut and press the fabric for the quilt. Press using a steam iron on the wool setting. Arrange the center squares, logs, and sashing on the design board.

## Building the Blocks

3. Build the 6 one-tier blocks clockwise, beginning with log 1, using a ½" seam allowance. Press each seam allowance away from the center as you piece the logs.

4. Topstitch around each center square, ¼" outside of the seam on each side, using a matching thread color. The topstitching helps define the patchwork and reinforces the seams, important for this design because you won't be quilting the pieced quilt top.

## Assembling the Quilt

5. Arrange the 6 center blocks into 2 rows of 3 blocks each to determine your favorite layout.

6. Using the row joining technique on page 32, join the individual blocks into rows, pressing the seam allowances in alternate directions.

7. Using the column sashing technique on page 33, join the first long strip of sashing with the top of the first row of blocks, using a ½" seam allowance. Join the second long strip of sashing with the bottom of the row in the same manner.

Continue to join the sashing to the rows until the quilt top is complete. Press the sashing seam allowances away from the blocks. Pin to catch the sashing seam allowances, and topstitch ¼" from the seam.

### Finishing the Quilt

8. Press the quilt top. Place the quilt top on the backing fabric, right sides together. Pin around the edges, leaving about 30" open on the bottom edge of the quilt for turning. (This quilt project does not use batting.)

9. Using a ½" seam allowance, stitch the perimeter of the quilt. Clip the corners at an angle and turn the quilt right side out, pressing it and opening the corners neatly with a pencil or chopstick.

10. Press the perimeter of the quilt, and pin the layers together every few inches. At the opening, fold in the fabric ½", pin, and press. Using a ¼" seam allowance and matching thread, topstitch around the entire perimeter of the quilt.

11. Now you'll mark your quilt top for hand-tying according to the Quilting Diagram. Because there is no batting, this quilt needs only a minimal tying structure. Knots are marked about every 18". You are ready to tie!

12. Use a curved needle and wool yarn to tie your quilt (page 36).

## TOPSTITCH "QUILTING"

Topstitching around a center square secures the layers of your quilt or project and achieves a decorative effect. It's perfect for projects with broadly pieced quilt tops that need added stability, such as the Winter Woolens Quilt and T-Shirt Memory Quilt (page 59). Topstitching follows the piecing structure of your project, much like outline quilting, however, the sewing is done before the quilt top has been completely assembled.

Press your blocks as usual and pin to catch the seam allowance where you want to add topstitching, typically just inside the center squares. Using a ¼" foot, topstitch along the piecing outline, making sure to catch the seam allowance.

# HOUSETOP **QUILT**

**Difficulty:** 🧵🧵🧵🧵🧵

**Type of block:** Housetop

**Techniques used:** outline quilting (page 35), echo quilting (page 35), binding (page 38)

This ultra-simple quilt is my tribute to the wonderful Housetop variation quilt designs made by some of the quilters of Gee's Bend. Women in this remote Alabama community have been making quilts for more than a century, and their quilts are truly works of art. Their Housetop patterns often use just one block, enlarged to fill the entire quilt. Inspired by their examples, I wanted to try my own version of a single-block, full-size quilt. After solving a few math problems, I had my own nine-fabric Housetop to share.

**Finished center:** 35″ x 44″

**Finished logs:** widths vary (Cutting Key)

**Finished block:** 96″ x 86″

**Number of blocks:** 1

**Finished quilt:** 96″ x 86″ (queen)

**You'll need:**

* 1 yard 45″ wide fabric for the center square
* Assorted quantities of 8 fabrics (Cutting Key, Logs)
* Batting, at least 98″ x 88″ (I used Quilter's Dream Green, which can be quilted up to 12″ apart.)
* Sheet or other backing fabric, at least 100″ x 90″
* ½ yard fabric for binding, if making your own, and 1″ binding-tape maker
* Thread (I used olive green for piecing, quilting, and binding)
* Fabric scraps, waste canvas, needle and embroidery thread, and hoop for signing the quilt (optional)

**NOTE:** To support the size and scale of this quilt's center and logs, piece the quilt top using a ½″ seam allowance.

| Cutting Key | A | Assorted |
| --- | --- | --- |
| **Center** | | |
| 36" x 45" | 1 | - |
| **Logs** | | |
| ① 13" x 36" | - | 1 |
| ② 15" x 58" | - | 1 |
| ③ 5" x 51" | - | 1 |
| ④ 15" x 63" | - | 1 |
| ⑤ 13" x 66" | - | 1 |
| ⑥ 10" x 76" | - | 1 |
| ⑦ 20" x 76" | - | 1 |
| ⑧ 10" x 94" | - | 1 |
| **Backing** | | |
| 100" x 90" | | |

**To make your own 1" binding:**

Cut and join 370" of 2"-wide strips (½ yard total fabric; I used the same fabric as my center square [A]).

Tip: You may need to join smaller pieces of fabric to make some of the logs for this project since they're large and wide.

## Cutting

1. Using the Assembly Diagrams as a guide, swatch or hold together fabrics you want to use and play with the arrangements until you find a combination of fabrics you like. I used a mix of olive green, white, brown, dark green, and coral prints for mine, with a large-scale print for the massive center square.

2. Using the Cutting Key, cut and press the fabric for the quilt. Place the center square and logs on the design board.

## Building the Block

3. Build the 2-tier block clockwise according to the Block Assembly Diagram, beginning with log 1, using a ½" seam allowance. Press each seam away from the center as you piece the logs.

## Finishing the Quilt

4. Press the quilt top. You're ready to mark your quilt top for quilting. This quilt uses 2 types of quilting, outline (which does not need to be marked) and echo. Mark the echo quilting lines: Measure and mark 2 rectangles inside the center square, one 6" and one 12" in from the square's edges, to echo the shape in smaller scales. Similarly, measure and mark rectangles inside logs 1, 2, 4, and 7, about 4" in from the edges of the logs.

**Assembly Diagrams**

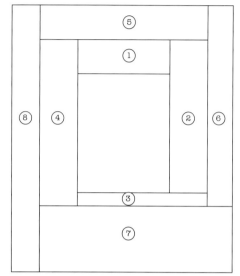

Block Assembly Diagram

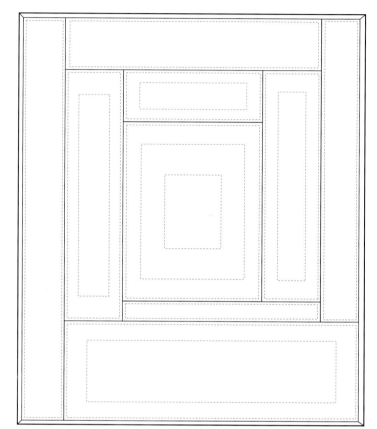

Front

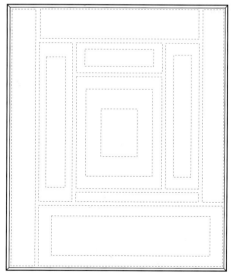

Back

5.  Make a quilt sandwich with the backing fabric, batting, and quilt top, and baste them together, making sure that the layers are smooth and even. You are ready to quilt!

6.  The first round of quilting is simple outline quilting. Quilt the center square first, topstitching a parallel line ½" inside the center square's boundaries. Then quilt each of the 9 logs in the same manner.

7.  The second round of quilting is echo quilting. Again starting from the center square, quilt along the quilting lines you marked in step 4.

8.  Square up the quilt sandwich. Baste around the perimeter edges.

9.  Make your own binding (page 38). If using premade binding, join the pieces as necessary. Bind the quilt to complete it.

## MAKING IT PERSONAL

Signing your quilt somewhere on the back, or anywhere you choose, is a lovely finishing gesture. You can write your name, date, location, the title, or any other details you like (for example, if the quilt is a gift, who the recipient is).

Using a permanent marker is the simplest method, but you can also write with fabric markers or quilting pencils and embroider over that. Signing is as individual as the quilt itself, so do whatever feels right to you.

For this quilt, you can create a simple house design using one or two of your log fabrics. Then sign it. I used waste canvas and coral thread to cross-stitch the year I made the quilt. Using the appliqué technique on page 40, attach the house to the back of your quilt, either before you baste the layers or after quilting and binding.

# T-SHIRT MEMORY **QUILT**

**Difficulty:** 🧵🧵🧵

**Type of block:** Picture Frame

**Techniques used:** scrap-piecing (page 27), spotlighting centers (page 28), column sashing (page 33), echo quilting (page 35), topstitch "quilting" (page 52)

I've collected T-shirts from crafty events for years and have always wanted to use them to make a quilt—a great way to remember all my friends who printed the shirts and my trips to other cities for craft fairs and meet-ups. A whole range of T-shirt fabrics mixed into one project can be a bit of a challenge to sew with, but this soft, cozy, instant-nostalgia quilt is worth every rolled edge and slippery pin!

If you've never sewn with knits, refer to Sewing with Jersey Fabric (page 62) for some tips to make the process easier.

**Finished centers:** 7" x 7" (Block 1), 10" x 10" (Block 2)

**Finished logs:** 3" (first tier), 1½" (second tier, Block 1 only)

**Finished block size:** 16" x 16"

**Number of blocks:** 9

**Finished quilt:** 62" x 62" (throw)

**You'll need:**

* 9 or 10 favorite T-shirts, depending on the size of your shirts and amount of usable fabric
* One queen-size jersey flat sheet for sashing and backing (A)
* Batting, at least 66" x 66" (I used Quilters Dream Green, which can be quilted up to 12" apart)
* 8" x 8" piece and 11" x 11" piece of pattern paper

**NOTE:** Use a ½" seam allowance for this project.

| Cutting Key | A | Assorted T-shirts |
|---|---|---|
| **Center Squares** | | |
| 8″ x 8″ (Block 1) | - | 4 |
| 11″ x 11″ (Block 2) | - | 5 |
| **Logs (Block 1)** | | |
| 4″ x 46″ total (pieced if necessary) | | 4 |
| 2½″ x 67″ total (pieced if necessary) | | 4 |
| **Logs (Block 2)** | | |
| 4″ x 58″ total (pieced if necessary) | | 5 |
| **Sashing** | | |
| 4″ x 17″ | 12 | - |
| 4″ x 64″ | 4 | - |
| **Backing** | | |
| 66″ x 66″ | 1 | - |

## Cutting

1. Looking at the designs on your T-shirts, select which ones should be featured in the small center squares (Block 1) and which in the large center squares (Block 2). Cut away the collars, cuffs, and other structural parts of the shirts to salvage as much useable fabric as possible. Cut the main body of the shirts up both sides, under the sleeves, to yield two larger flat pieces—the front and back of each shirt.

2. Using the Cutting Key, cut and press the fabric for the center squares, sashing, and backing. Use the pattern paper and the spotlighting centers technique to cut out the 9 center squares. Set aside the sashing and backing fabric.

3. Arrange the center squares with the remaining T-shirt fabric on the design board until you find combinations of fabrics that you like. Then cut and press the logs according to the Cutting Key, piecing if necessary to get the needed length. Place the logs with the center squares on the design board according to the assembly diagrams for Blocks 1 and 2. You should have 4 versions of Block 1 and 5 versions of Block 2.

## Building the Blocks

4. Build the 2-tier blocks (Block 1). Piece the first tier of the blocks clockwise, using a ½″ seam allowance, according to the Block 1 Assembly Diagram. Press the seam allowances away from the center. Pin to catch the seams, and topstitch ¼″ outside the logs, as shown on the assembly diagram. using a complementary thread color. The topstitching helps define the patchwork and

# Assembly Diagrams

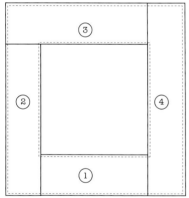

Block Assembly Diagram – 1
(with topstitching)

Block Assembly Diagram – 2
(with topstitching)

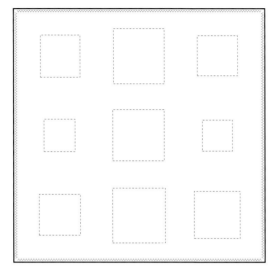

Back

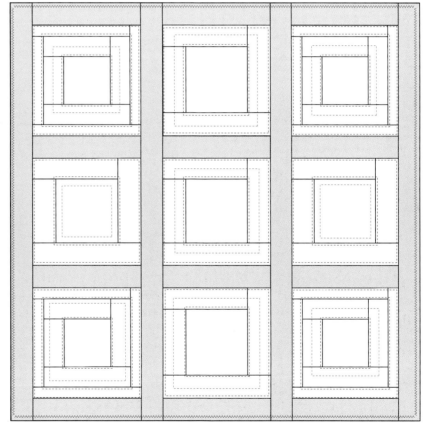

Front

-------- topstitching
-------- quilting

gives strength to the soft, flexible fabric.

Repeat to piece, press, and topstitch the second tier of logs.

**5.** Build the one-tier blocks (Block 2). Piece, press, and topstitch all 5 blocks in the same manner as the blocks in step 4.

### Assembling the Quilt

**6.** When you've completed all 9 blocks, press them neatly, and arrange them on the design board in 3 rows of 3 blocks each, moving the blocks around to determine your favorite layout. I placed my Block 2 blocks in a cross formation with my Block 1 blocks at the 4 corners. Place the sashing between the rows and columns of blocks.

**7.** Using the column sashing technique on page 33 and a ½" seam allowance, join the first column of blocks with strips of 17" sashing, beginning and ending the column with sashing strips. Press the seams open. Pin to catch the seams, and topstitch using a complementary thread color.

Join the second and third columns in the same manner, pressing and topstitching each column when you complete it.

**8.** Now join a strip of 64" vertical sashing to the left side of the first column, using a ½" seam allowance. Press the seam open, and topstitch the length of the column along the sashing, catching the seam in the stitching. Then join your first and second columns with vertical sashing, using a ½" seam allowance, and pressing, pinning, and topstitching in the same manner.

### SEWING WITH JERSEY FABRIC

Sewing knit jersey fabrics is more challenging than sewing quilting cottons, as jersey tends to slip, roll, stretch, and shift. This project is not necessarily made for perfectionists! Fabric amounts and measurements can vary slightly due to the stretchy nature of the fabric. But don't let this fabric intimidate you. With a little extra care, you'll be on your way to mastering jersey—and you'll have a whole new fabric stash to choose from for future projects. Here are some tips:

* Piece together jersey of the same weight whenever possible.
* Use a ½" seam allowance for piecing and sashing to accommodate the rolls and shifts in fabric.
* Press often when piecing to help control the fabric edges.
* Sew slowly and carefully, and change the machine needle frequently. I recommend a universal or ball-point needle to make the stitching smoother and easier.

Repeat to join your second and third columns. Then join the remaining strip of vertical sashing to the right side of the joined columns in the same manner. This is your T-shirt quilt top!

## Finishing the Quilt

9. Press the quilt top. You're ready to mark your quilt for quilting. This quilt uses an echo quilting pattern (page 35). With a quilting ruler and washable marker, mark squares on each of the 9 blocks following the pattern shown on the quilting diagram. Blocks 1 and 2 have different quilting patterns, as shown.

10. Press the backing fabric quilt top. Lay out your batting and place the backing fabric on top, right side up. Pin the layers in place around the perimeter edges and baste together, using a scant ⅛" seam allowance.

11. Place the quilt top on the backing fabric, right sides together. Pin around the edges, leaving about 30" open along the bottom edge of the quilt for turning.

12. Using a ½" seam allowance, stitch the perimeter of the quilt. Do not stitch the opening closed.

**NOTE:** If you find it impossible to maintain a perfectly even seam allowance, don't worry. You can always go back and resew places where the seam wavers too much. Jersey fabric is very forgiving.

13. Square up the quilt sandwich. Clip the corners at an angle and turn the quilt right side out, trying not to stretch the quilt top. Shake the quilt a few times so the layers smooth into place. The jersey will cling nicely to the batting.

14. Press the perimeter of the quilt and pin every few inches. At the opening, turn in the unfinished edge ½". Set your machine to a long, wide zigzag stitch. Using matching thread, stitch around the perimeter of the quilt 1" in from the edge. Although a zigzag edging is not as neat as a beautifully pressed and sewn binding, it complements the flexible nature of jersey fabric.

15. With a complementary thread color, quilt the echo quilting pattern. Your cozy quilt is done!

# MODERN CROSSES QUILT

**Difficulty:** 🪡🪡🪡🪡🪡

**Type of block:** Sunshine and Shadow

**Techniques used:** chain-piecing (page 31), row joining (page 32), column joining (page 32), machine-tying (page 37), binding (page 38), button embellishment (page 40)

This design pares down log cabin piecing to its most basic elements—a center square and four logs in Sunshine and Shadow style. The way you orient the blocks creates a repeating modern cross design across the quilt. Each cross, embellished with a sweet vintage button, is made by joining four blocks together. Offsetting the rows of crosses in a stair-step pattern brings the simple shapes and lines to life.

**Finished center:** 1¾" x 1¾"

**Finished logs:** 1½" wide

**Finished block:** four 4¾" x 4¾" blocks joined into a Modern Cross Block of 9½" x 9½"

**Number of blocks:** 240 joined to make 60 Modern Cross Blocks

**Binding:** 330" (9¼ yards) of 1" finished binding, handmade or purchased

**Finished quilt:** 80" x 80" (small full)

## You'll need:
* 8¼ yards solid-colored quilting cotton, 4 yards for the front and 4¼ for the back (A) (I used Kona Cotton in Snow from Robert Kaufman Fabrics)
* Scraps of 60 prints, 2" x 25" each
* Plastic bags
* ⅓ yard fabric for pieced backing design (C )
* Batting, at least 84" x 84" (I used Quilters Dream Puff, which can be quilted up to 10" apart)
* ½ yard fabric for binding, or use leftover assorted fabrics from log strips to make a patchwork binding (Cutting Key, Note), and 1" binding-tape maker
* 60 machine-washable buttons

| Cutting Key | A | C | Assorted |
|---|---|---|---|
| **Center Squares** | | | |
| 2¼" x 2¼" | 240 | - | - |
| **Logs** | | | |
| 2" x 35" | 60 | - | - |
| 2" x 25" | - | - | 60 (assorted fabrics) |

**NOTE:** If making your own patchwork binding, cut at least 17 of your assorted-fabric log strips in 44" lengths and set aside any leftover scraps to scrap-piece the binding.

| Cutting Key | A | C | Assorted |
|---|---|---|---|
| **Row Ends** | | | |
| 5¼" x 10" | 8 | - | - |
| **BACKING** | | | |
| **Center Squares** | | | |
| 6¾" x 6¾" | 4 | - | - |
| **Logs** | | | |
| 6" x 44" | 3 | - | - |
| 6" x 44" | - | 2 | - |
| **Backing Pieces** | | | |
| 22" x 40" | 2 | - | - |
| 22" x 84" | 2 | - | - |

**To make your own 1" binding:**

Cut and join 360" of 2"-wide strips (½ yard total fabric; I used 17 leftover 44" strips from my assorted log fabrics).

## Cutting

1. Using the Front Quilt Assembly Diagram as a guide, swatch or hold together fabrics you want to use and play with the arrangements until you find a combination of fabrics you like. I used a fun mix of scraps and remnants from my stash—60 different prints in all.

2. Using the Cutting Key, cut and press the fabric for the quilt. Separate the solid-color logs and 5¼" x 10" Row End rectangles in plastic bags, away from the print logs. Set aside the backing fabric.

## Building the Blocks

3. Chain-piece 4 center squares to a strip of patterned fabric. This fabric will become the first log in these blocks. Trim the logs and press. Chain-piece the joined center/log pieces to the leftover

## Assembly Diagrams

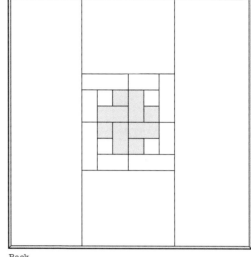

4-Block Assembly Diagram

Back

Block Assembly
Diagram

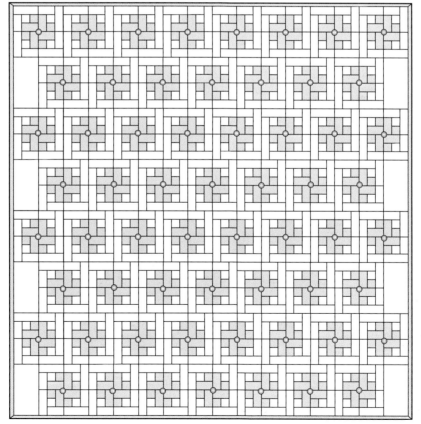

Front

fabric strip, so that logs 1 and 2 are the same fabric. Trim and press. You'll use about 25" of printed fabric.

4. Chain-piece the blocks to a solid-color strip of fabric in the same manner. The solid fabric will become the logs 3 and 4 in these blocks. You'll use about 35" of solid fabric.

5. Press the blocks neatly. Using the four-way row joining technique on page 32, join the blocks so the printed fabric logs align to form a cross shape at the center of the 4 blocks. Press. This is your first Modern Cross Block!

6. Repeat steps 2–4 to make the remaining 59 Modern Cross Blocks.

### Assembling the Quilt Front

7. When you've completed all 60 Modern Cross Blocks, press them neatly, and arrange them on the design board in 8 rows of crosses. I suggest an offset layout with 7 cross blocks in the first row, 8 blocks in the second, and so on. From top to bottom, you'll have an 8-7-8-7-8-7-8-7 alternation.

8. Place one of the Row End rectangles at the beginning and end of each 7-block row to make all rows equal in length.

9. Join the first row of cross blocks and rectangles using the column piecing technique on page 32 (think of the row as your column, just turned on its side). Press. Join the remaining rows of cross blocks and sashing, pressing each row when you complete it.

## IN A BIND

When piecing a binding from multiple fabrics with lots of patterns and colors, many quilters choose to sew the pieces together with straight, rather than angled, seams. These straight seams will calm down the active movement from one wildly patterned fabric to another. For my Modern Crosses Quilt, I used seventeen patterned fabric strips left over from building the blocks and sewed them together using a ¼" straight seam allowance.

**10.** Now join your first and second rows, matching seams so that the crosses are staggered with one another as shown in the Quilt Front Diagram. The block seams should match up neatly. Press the row seam toward the bottom.

Repeat to join your second, third, and fourth rows, pressing each row seam when you complete it, to form one half of the quilt top. Then join your eighth, seventh, sixth, and fifth rows in the same manner to form the second half.

**11.** Join the 2 halves of the quilt top and press the center seam. Your quilt top is complete!

## Assembling the Quilt Back

**12.** Now it's time to piece the quilt's backing, which is made up of 1 large Modern Cross Block centered on a solid-colored backing fabric. Using the center squares and logs you cut for the backing, follow steps 3–5 to piece and join 4 blocks to make 1 large-scale Modern Cross Block.

**13.** Pin and sew one 40"-long piece of backing fabric to one short side of the large cross block, according to the Quilt Back Diagram. Repeat with the remaining 40"-long piece of backing fabric on the other short side of the cross block. Press the seams away from the center of the cross block.

**14.** Pin and sew the 84"-long pieces of backing fabric to the long edges of the joined cross block/backing fabric. Press the seams away from center of the cross block. Your backing is complete!

## Finishing the Quilt

**15.** Press the quilt top. Make a quilt sandwich with your pieced backing fabric, batting, and quilt top, and baste together, making sure that the layers are smooth and even.

**16.** Machine-tie each cross at the center. You can move the quilt between ties to knot several quilt blocks at a time before trimming threads.

**17.** Square up the quilt sandwich and baste around the perimeter edge. Bind the quilt with hand-made patchwork binding to complete.

**18.** Select favorite new or vintage washable buttons and hand-sew them over each machine-tie, using the button embellishment technique. I mixed a variety of buttons in contrasting colors that suited the crosses and the patchwork binding.

# VINTAGE LINENS **QUILT**

**Difficulty:** 🧵🧵🧵

**Type of block:** Random

**Techniques used:** scrap-piecing (page 27), spotlighting centers (page 28), chain-piecing (page 31), column sashing (page 33), adding borders (page 34), diagonal quilting (page 35), binding (page 38)

I love pretty vintage sheets and pillowcases, and I collect them at estate sales and thrift stores—they provide so much fabric at low cost, making them perfect for cutting up, mixing, and matching. I used more than two dozen prints in this exuberant, random log cabin design. Because I wanted a lively, busy feel to my quilt, I sashed the colorful blocks with a cheater print that imitates the look of patchwork. Using a solid color or a more static sashing fabric will give your quilt a calmer feel.

**Finished center:** 4″ x 4″

**Finished logs:** 1½″ wide

**Finished block:** 13″ x 13″

**Number of blocks:** 25

**Binding:** about 330″ (9¼ yards) of 1″ binding, handmade or purchased

**Finished quilt:** 84″ x 84″ (small full)

**You'll need:**

* 23 fat quarters, pillowcases, or reclaimed linens in different prints, each at least 18″ x 22″
* 1 twin-size flat or fitted sheet for sashing, at least 44″ x 60″ (A)
* 1 queen-size flat sheet for the backing and binding, at least 88″ x 98″ (B), and 1″ binding-tape maker
* Batting, at least 86″ x 86″ (I used Quilters Dream Cotton Request, which can be quilted up to 8″ apart)
* 4½″ x 4½″ piece of pattern paper, for spotlighting centers
* 4½″ x 4½″ piece of cardboard, optional
* Plastic bags
* Thread (I used white for piecing and sashing, yellow for quilting, and blue for binding)

**NOTES:**

* Soft vintage linens may have some waviness and puffiness, almost as though the fabric were cut on the bias. A lofty, thick batting will hide these irregularities better than a thin batting. As always, adapt the spacing of your quilting lines to accommodate the type of batting you choose.
* When sourcing vintage fabric, look for fat-quarter sets of vintage sheets on Etsy.com. I used one set of 10 fat quarters, along with 15 pillowcases, sheets, and remnants. To use fewer fabrics, simply repeat fabrics more frequently in your quilt top. Just be sure that you have the same total amount of fabric needed.

| Cutting Key | A | B | Assorted |
|---|---|---|---|
| **Center Squares** | | | |
| 4½" x 4½" | 1 | 1 | 23 |
| **Logs** | | | |
| 2" x 130" total (pieced if necessary) | 1 | 1 | 23 |
| **Sashing and Borders** | | | |
| 3" x 44" (pieced if necessary) | 21 | - | - |

**NOTE:** For sashing and borders, you'll need 900" total of 3"-wide fabric strips.

| Backing | | | |
|---|---|---|---|
| 88" x 88" | - | 1 | - |

**To make your own 1" binding tape:**

Cut and join 330" of 2"-wide strips (½ yard total fabric); I used the same fabric as my backing [B].

## Cutting

1. Using the Quilt Assembly Diagram as a guide, choose 23 vintage sheets, pillowcases, or smaller sections (such as fat quarters) to mix together in a random pattern. I chose mostly florals and bright or pastel colors. Choose two other vintage sheets to use for center squares, logs, sashing, and backing, for a total of 25.

2. Using the Cutting Key, cut and press the fabric for the quilt. Use the pattern paper and the spotlighting centers technique to cut out the 25 center squares first, and then cut the logs. Divide the logs by general color family and put each group into a large plastic bag: I grouped my fabrics into pinks, blues, yellows and oranges, and whites/lights. You can cut your sashing and borders now, or wait until your blocks are finished to choose what patterned or solid fabric you'll use.

**NOTE:** When cutting out large numbers of center squares, I find it easiest to use a piece of cardboard as a template, then cut the fabric using a rotary cutter on a cutting mat (page 27).

## Building the Blocks

3. I used a technique I call intentional randomness to build my blocks. Choose 4 center squares and 4 strips of fabric from the plastic bags. Piece each center square to a different strip to build the first logs in the blocks. Trim and press. You have begun 4 blocks.

**Assembly Diagrams**

Block Assembly Diagram

Front

4.  Continue choosing strips of fabric to add as logs and center squares to begin new blocks, chain-piecing blocks in varying stages of completion to the fabric strips. The same fabric strip will become a different log in each block. This method of chain-piecing ensures uniquely pieced blocks (Chain-Piecing for Variety, page 75). Chain-piece and press center squares and logs to make 25 blocks.

    **NOTE:** Save your scraps to scrap-piece logs if needed.

### Assembling the Quilt

5.  When you've completed all 25 blocks, press them neatly, and arrange them on the design board out in 5 rows of 5 columns each, moving the blocks around to determine your favorite layout. If you're still choosing your sashing and borders from several patterned or solid choices, place a few blocks on the different fabrics and see what appeals most. A solid or quieter pattern will make each individual block stand out more in the quilt design than a busy pattern. After choosing your fabric, cut as directed in the Cutting Key.

6.  Using the column sashing technique on page 33, join the first column of 5 blocks with strips of sashing. Press. Join the remaining columns, pressing each column when you complete it.

7.  Now join your first and second columns with vertical sashing, and repeat to join your second, third, fourth and fifth columns. Press.

8.  Using the adding borders technique on page 34, add the border strips to complete the quilt top, piecing if necessary. Press.

## Finishing the Quilt

**9.** Press the quilt top. You're ready to mark your quilt top for quilting. This quilt uses a diagonal quilting pattern (page 35). Mark diagonal lines at a 45-degree angle to the sides of your center squares, from upper left to bottom right for a total of 18 diagonal lines.

**10.** Make a quilt sandwich with your backing fabric, batting, and quilt top and baste them together, making sure all layers are smooth and even. You are ready to quilt!

**11.** With a complementary thread color, begin to quilt the diagonal quilting lines. Quilt from the center of the quilt out toward the edges.

**12.** Square up the quilt sandwich and baste around the perimeter edge. Bind the quilt to complete.

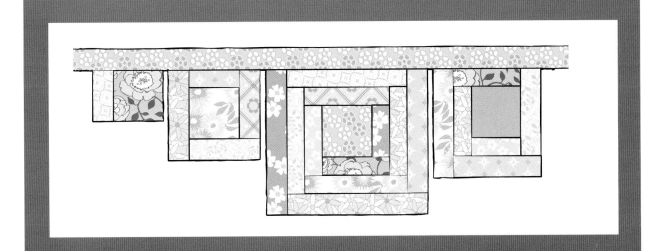

## CHAIN-PIECING FOR VARIETY

To keep the mix of fabrics interesting and varied when chain-piecing, consider sewing a fabric strip to more than one block in different log positions. One strip of chain-pieced fabric might become logs 2, 5, 12, and 7 in four different blocks. When you've added a new log to a block, you can either continue piecing that block, adding the next log, or set the block aside as you piece other blocks that are in various stages of completion. As blocks are pieced, add more center squares to start building additional blocks. This way, you'll maintain variety of fabric from block to block.

In the Vintage Linens Quilt, I pieced two to five blocks at a time, depending on how I wanted to use each fabric strip. The one rule I followed when planning each block was to use the center fabric as a log in the second or third tier of the block to achieve an echo effect. Otherwise I didn't duplicate prints in the same block, so no like fabrics ever touched.

# BRIGHT FURROWS **QUILT**

**Difficulty:** 🧵🧵🧵

**Type of block:** Sunshine and Shadow

**Techniques used:** chain-piecing (page 31), four-way (row) joining (page 32), geometric quilting (page 35), binding (page 38)

I found out that I was expecting our second baby while I was writing this book, so this bright, happy quilt was the first thing I ever made for him. I sized it up generously from a traditional crib quilt, so he'd still be able to use it as a preschooler, or take it out to the backyard with plenty of room to play with toys. I loved mixing in colorful little prints like the strawberries, mushrooms, stripes, dots, and keys, and came up with a simple way to randomize my block piecing so each of the 36 blocks used each of the twelve fabrics exactly once—drawing the eye up and down the dramatic diagonals of the straight furrows.

**Finished centers:** 1¼"

**Finished logs:** 1¼" wide

**Finished block:** 9"

**Number of blocks:** 36

**Finished quilt:** 54" x 54"
(large baby quilt/throw)

**You'll need:**

* ⅛ yard fabric for center squares in your dominant color (I used a solid yellow quilting cotton)
* ⅓ yard each of six assorted prints and solids in your dominant color (I used yellows, including some of the same solid fabric as my centers)
* ¼ yard each of six assorted prints and solids in your recessive color (I used aquas)

* ½ yard of a fabric in a dominant color for backing square and binding—depending on joining, you may need the lesser amount of fabric (I used a tiny mushroom print)
* 2¼ yards of a fabric in a recessive color for backing logs (I used a larger bright abstract print)
* Batting, at least 56" square (I used Nature-Fil organic cotton-and-bamboo batting that could be quilted up to 8" apart)
* Thread (I used yellow to complement my dominant logs and match my binding fabric)
* 1" binding-tape maker (recommended)

**NOTE:** In this design, the fabric color you use for logs 1 and 2 (and beyond on outer tiers) is described as "recessive," and the fabric color you use for center squares and logs 3 and 4 (and beyond) is described as "dominant." This is because in the finished Straight Furrows design, the dominant diagonal sections will be wider than the recessive ones, due to the varied log lengths, and the centers blending into the dominant sections.

| Cutting Key | Assorted Dominant | Assorted Recessive |
|---|---|---|
| **Center Squares** | | |
| 1¾" x 1¾" | 36 | - |

NOTE: Center squares can be cut from two extra 1¾" x 44" strips from your dominant colors.

| | | |
|---|---|---|
| **Logs** | | |
| 1¾" x 44" | | 5 each of 6 assorted aqua prints and solids (A-F) |
| 1¾" x 44" | 6 each of 6 assorted yellow prints and solids (G-L) | |
| **BACKING** | | |
| **Center Square** | | |
| 19" x 19" | 1 | - |
| **Logs** | | |
| 20" x 44" | - | 4 |

Join leftover strips of fabric to create logs as needed, a total of approximately 150 inches.

**To make your own 1" binding:**

Cut and join 230" of 2"-wide strips (¼ yard total fabric) in a dominant color print.

## Cutting

1. Choose six compatible fabrics in each of two color families you like together—I decided on a mix of solids and small prints in a close range of bright aquas and yellows, including many different quilting cottons, a shot cotton, and a batik. You'll use one of your dominant colors as your center square fabric, and another one as your backing center square and binding. You'll use one of your recessive color fabrics for your wide backing logs, too. Swatch all your fabrics and pin them to a piece of paper, or make a tally sheet of your dozen dominant and recessive fabrics to keep them organized. I listed my 6 different aquas and 6 different yellows for reference, describing each one as "batik," "keys," "dark solid," "large dot," and so on.

2. Using the Cutting Key, cut and press the fabric for the quilt. Cut your center squares from the two extra strips of one of the dominant fabrics you've chosen.

## Building the Blocks

3. Divide your 36 center squares into 6 groups of 6. Chain-piece each stack of 6 squares to one of the 6 different recessive fabric strips (working in list or swatch order may make this easier) until all 36 centers have the first log joined. Press and trim each one.

# Assembly Diagrams

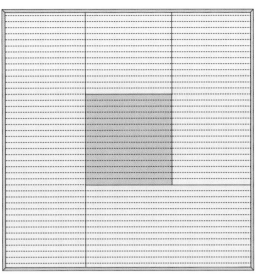

Block Assembly Diagram

Back

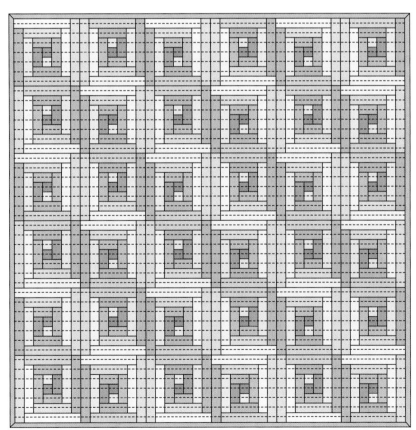

Front

4. Shuffle your blocks into new stacks of 6 so that you add a different recessive fabric to each one as log 2 (ie, no repeating a fabric in a block that already has that one as a first log). I found the easiest way to do this was to look for what I hadn't already used and sort the blocks in progress that way. Mix the stacks up a bit so that they don't repeat each fabric in the same order as you go. I arranged my blocks on my ironing board, making space to build my six new stacks in my tally list order along the length of it, and pinned each stack together so they wouldn't get jumbled together in the piecing steps.

5. Chain-piece your first stack of blocks to its new log, then the second stack to its new log, and so on until all 36 blocks have their second logs attached. Press and cut them.

6. Now shuffle your blocks again so you have a random mix and divide them into stacks of 6. Chain-piece each stack to a different dominant fabric in list order, press, and cut them—this is log 3.

**NOTE:** The only fabric overlap you'll have throughout this quilt top is reusing the same center square fabric in one log in each block.

7. Shuffle your blocks again and add log 4 the same way. You have completed the first tier of logs (of the three tiers that will complete each block), with no overlaps!

8. Shuffling blocks into new stacks of 6 each time, and referring to your list or swatches to remember which fabrics you're adding next, add logs 5 and 6 using recessive fabrics.

9. Add logs 7 and 8 the same way, but in dominant fabrics.

10. By now your shuffling will need to get a little more deliberate, as you'll have fewer and fewer blocks that don't use each certain fabric yet—just 12 and then 6 of each for this last tier of recessive and dominant logs. When you make your stacks now, you will probably need to rearrange some blocks into other stacks as you go, to maintain the only-new-logs rule. Pinning each stack together, and continuing to work in list order, helped me keep my blocks organized. Add logs 9 and 10 in new recessive and 11 and 12 in new dominant fabrics. Press each block well—you are ready to arrange them into your quilt top!

11. Arrange your blocks 6 by 6 on a flannel design wall or floor to create the Straight Furrows pattern. Switch blocks around if they have matching fabrics touching on their outer log tiers, so you have a nice mix of randomized prints and solids throughout. Take a photo for reference if you like.

### Assembling the Quilt

12. Using the 4-way joining technique, begin joining your upper left-hand group of four blocks, matching corners and edges neatly. Press the 4-block group well. Continue until you've joined 9 groups of 4 blocks, 3 in each row—each one will look identical when joined, patternwise.

13. Join your top row of three of the joined blocks in 1-2-3 order, and continue to join the middle and bottom row the same way as well. Press the seams well.

14. Finally, you'll join your three long rows of blocks (each one will be 6 blocks wide and 2 blocks tall) to finish your quilt top. Press all joining seams neatly.

**15.** Now you'll make the backing design. Join your first recessive-color 20″ log to the 19″ dominant-color center square, using a ½-inch seam allowance and piecing clockwise since the pieces are so large, and press. Continue to add logs 2, 3, and 4, joining strips of the log fabric to achieve length when necessary. Press well.

## Finishing the Quilt

**16.** Make a quilt sandwich with your backing, batting, and quilt top. Baste the layers together, making sure that they are smooth and even. You are ready to quilt!

**17.** This quilt uses a simple geometric quilting pattern of horizontal lines bisecting each log across the neighboring blocks, as shown on the Front Diagram. It does not need to be marked—you can follow the edges of the logs in each of the blocks, evenly spacing your quilting lines halfway between them.

**18.** Beginning in the center section of the quilt, quilt the horizontal lines from side to side. Continue, checking the back to make sure it lies even and smooth, until you have finished the entire quilt.

**19.** Square up the quilt sandwich and baste around the perimeter edge. Bind the quilt to complete it.

# CLOUDS IN THE SKY **DUVET COVER**

**Difficulty:** 🧵🧵🧵🧵

**Type of block:** Sunshine and Shadow

**Techniques used:** chain-piecing (page 31), row joining (page 32), column joining (page 32), adding borders (page 34), stitch-in-the-ditch quilting (page 35), double-fold hem (page 40)

This quilt was inspired by the weather here in Portland—our months of calm, cool, rainy days are punctuated with sudden sunny moments. Seeing the patches of bright blue and feeling the sun's warmth is such a pick-me-up on a long, dark, gray afternoon, and that was the feeling I wanted to capture in this version of the traditional Sunshine and Shadow log cabin style. I made this project as a simple duvet cover for our every-day down comforter, but you can easily adapt it into a traditional bound quilt if you prefer.

**Finished centers:** 1¾" x 1¾"

**Finished logs:** 1" wide

**Finished block:** 9¾" x 9¾"

**Number of blocks:** 48

**Finished quilt:** 92" x 80" (queen/king duvet cover)

**You'll need:**

* ¼ yard off-white fabric for center squares (I used Kona Cotton in Snow from Robert Kaufman Fabrics) (I)
* ⅓ yard very light aqua fabric (A)
* 2½ yards very light gray fabric for borders, plus ½ yard (B)
* ½ yard light aqua fabric (C)
* ⅔ yard light gray fabric (D)
* ⅔ yard medium aqua fabric (E)
* ¾ yard medium gray fabric (F)
* 1 yard dark aqua fabric (G)
* 1 yard dark gray fabric (H)
* Batting, at least 96" x 84" (I used Quilters Dream Green, which can be quilted up to 12" apart)
* Sheet or other inner backing fabric, at least 96" x 84"
* Sheet or other outer backing fabric, at least 96" x 84"
* Thread in off-white and gray

For optional binding (traditional quilt only):
* ½ yard fabric for binding and 1" binding-tape maker; or 9¾ yards purchased binding

| Cutting Key | A | B | C | D | E | F | G | H | I |
|---|---|---|---|---|---|---|---|---|---|
| **Center Squares** | | | | | | | | | |
| 2¼" x 2¼" | - | - | - | - | - | - | - | - | 48 |
| **Logs** | | | | | | | | | |
| 1½" x 44" | 7 | - | - | - | - | - | - | - | - |
| 1½" x 44" | - | 9 | - | - | - | - | - | - | - |
| 1½" x 44" | - | - | 12 | - | - | - | - | - | - |
| 1½" x 44" | - | - | - | 14 | - | - | - | - | - |
| 1½" x 44" | - | - | - | - | 16 | - | - | - | - |
| 1½" x 44" | - | - | - | - | - | 18 | - | - | - |
| 1½" x 44" | - | - | - | - | - | - | 20 | - | - |
| 1½" x 44" | - | - | - | - | - | - | - | 23 | - |

**NOTE:** To conserve fabric, join leftover strips of fabric to create logs for the outer tiers as needed.

| | | | | | | | | | |
|---|---|---|---|---|---|---|---|---|---|
| **Borders** | | | | | | | | | |
| 11" x 81" (pieced if necessary) | - | 1 | - | - | - | - | - | - | - |
| 11" x 89" (pieced if necessary) | - | 1 | - | - | - | - | - | - | - |
| 7" x 72" (pieced if necessary) | - | 1 | - | - | - | - | - | - | - |
| 7" x 84" (pieced if necessary) | - | 1 | - | - | - | - | - | - | - |
| **Inner Backing** | | | | | | | | | |
| 96" x 84" | | | | | | | | | |
| **Outer Backing** | | | | | | | | | |
| 96" x 84" | | | | | | | | | |

**NOTE:** To get the most out of your fabric, cut the border strips parallel to the selvage. You can cut each of these four border pieces from one 2½-yard section of fabric, side by side.

**To make your own 1" binding** (for a traditional bound quilt only):

Cut and join 360" of 2"-wide strips (½ yard total fabric).

## Cutting

1. Using the Block Assembly Diagram as a guide, swatch or hold together fabrics you want to use and play with the arrangements until you find a combination of fabrics you like. As noted in the materials list, I used aqua and gray fabrics in several values.

2. Using the Cutting Key, cut and press the fabric for the quilt. Set the border strips aside.

## Assembly Diagrams

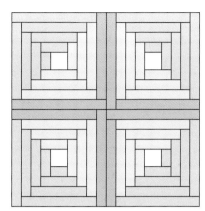

Block Assembly Diagram

4-Block Assembly Diagram

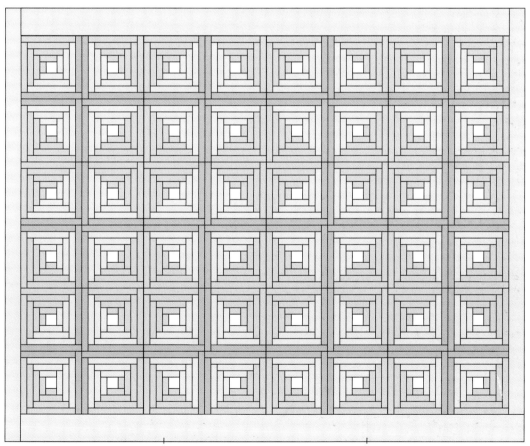

Front

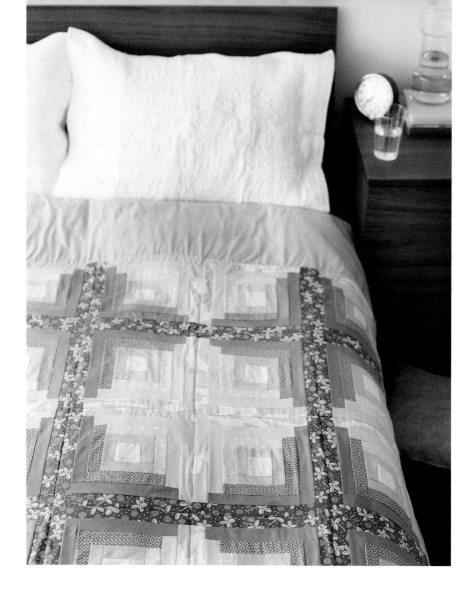

### Building the Blocks

**3.** Chain-piece all of your center squares to strips of fabric (A). This fabric will become the first logs in these blocks. Trim the logs and press. Chain-piece the joined center/log pieces to strips of fabric (A), so that logs 1 and 2 are the same fabric. Trim and press.

**4.** Chain-piece the blocks to fabric (B) in the same manner to piece logs 3 and 4, to fabric (C) to piece logs 5 and 6, to fabric (D) to piece logs 7 and 8, to fabric (E) to piece logs 9 and 10, to fabric (F) to piece logs 11 and 12, to fabric (G) to piece logs 13 and 14, and to fabric (H) to piece logs 15 and 16. Trim and press your blocks after each new log is added.

### Assembling the Duvet Cover

**5.** When you've completed all 48 blocks, press them neatly, and arrange them on the design board in 6 rows of 8 blocks each, as shown on the Front Assembly Diagram. Position blocks in groups of 4 with logs 15 and 16 meeting to achieve a gray-dominant design, or with logs 13 and 14 meeting to achieve an aqua-dominant design. You will have 12 groups of 4 blocks.

6.  Using the four-way row joining technique on page 32, join each group of 4 blocks. Place the 12 groups on the design board in 3 rows of 4 four-block units.

7.  Join the first row of four-block units using the column piecing technique on page 32 (think of the row as your column, just turned on its side). Press, alternating the direction of the seam. Join the remaining rows of four-block units, pressing each row when you complete it.

8.  Now join your first and second rows, matching seams so that the crosses are aligned as in the Front Diagram. Press the seam joining rows toward the bottom of the quilt.

    Repeat to join your second, third, and fourth rows, pressing each column seam when you complete it.

9.  Using the adding borders technique on page 34, add the border strips to complete the quilt top, piecing if necessary. Press.

## Finishing the Duvet Cover

10. Press the quilt top and inner backing fabric. Make a quilt sandwich with your inner backing fabric (wrong side up), batting, and quilt top. Baste together using at least 2 pins or tabs per block, making sure that the layers are smooth and even. You are ready to quilt!

**NOTE:** If you prefer to make a traditional bound quilt instead of a duvet cover, this quilt sandwich will form your final, complete quilt.

11. This quilt uses the stitch-in-the-ditch quilting pattern (page 35), which does not need to be marked. Quilting in the center area of the quilt first, work vertically and horizontally to outline all 48 blocks.

12. Square up the quilt sandwich and baste around the perimeter edge.

13. Measure and mark an opening for the duvet cover about 38″ long, centered along the bottom edge of the quilt top. Measure and mark another 38″-long opening, centered on one long edge of the outer backing fabric. Press and sew a ½″ double-fold hem for the backing fabric's opening, leaving the rest of the perimeter unsewn for now.

14. Place the quilted top on the outer backing fabric, right sides together matching the long openings. Pin around the edges, leaving the 38″-opening unpinned.

15. Using a ½″ seam allowance, stitch around the perimeter of the quilt. Clip the corners at an angle and trim any excess fabric (again leaving the opening alone), if necessary. Turn the duvet cover right side out, pressing it and opening the corners neatly with a pencil or chopstick.

16. At the opening of the duvet cover, roll the raw edge of the quilted cover under with its batting layer inside, pinning it evenly in place so the raw edge is tucked inside the roll. Using a modified version of the double-fold hem technique, stitch the quilted top all along the wrong side of the 38″ opening. I chose to hand-sew the top edge of the opening on my duvet cover using a simple whipstitch on the wrong side. You are ready to place your king- or queen-sized comforter inside its pretty new cover, and stay cozy on those gray winter days!

# NORTHWEST MODERN **QUILT**

**Difficulty:** 🧵🧵🧵🧵🧵

**Type of block:** Color Story

DESIGNED BY DANIELA CAINE

**Techniques used:** row joining (page 32), stitch-in-the-ditch quilting (page 35), outline quilting (page 35), geometric quilting (page 35), binding (page 38), topstitching (page 52)

This bold, graphic design shows off a log cabin structure enclosing a log cabin quilt. The "center square" is pieced from twelve smaller log cabin blocks, then border strips mimic large "logs" around it. This asymmetrical, eye-catching look gives a modern spin to the wonderfully simplistic log cabin quilt construction.

**Finished center:** 5″ x 15″

**Finished logs:** widths vary (Cutting Key)

**Number of blocks:** 12

**Binding:** about 370″ (10¼ yards) of 1″ finished binding, handmade or purchased

**Finished quilt:** 96″ x 86″ (full/queen)

**You'll need:**

* 2 yards purple fabric (A)
* 3 yards off-white fabric (B)
* 8½ yards brown fabric (C), for quilt top, binding, and backing (3½ yards needed for quilt top only)
* Batting, 98″ x 89″ (I used Quilters Dream Green, which can be quilted up to 12″ apart)
* 98″ x 89″ of muslin (often found in the upholstery section of fabric stores)

**NOTE:** If you do not wish to piece the backing, simply substitute a backing fabric for the pieced backing and don't use the muslin (Double Your Quilts, page 93).

* Thread to match fabrics (A–C) and muslin
* 1″ binding-tape maker (recommended)

| Cutting Key | A<br>Purple | B<br>Off-White | C<br>Brown |
|---|---|---|---|
| **Center Square** | | | |
| 5" x 15¼" | 12 | - | - |
| **Logs** | | | |
| 5" x 6½" (1) | - | 7 | 5 |
| 3" x 21" (2) | - | 12 | - |
| 3" x 7½" (3) | - | 5 | 7 |
| 7" x 24½" (4) | - | 12 | - |
| **Border Strips** | | | |
| 2" x 135" (1 and 2) | 2 | - | - |
| 6¼" x 63" (3) | 1 | - | - |
| 7" x 81" (4) | 1 | - | - |
| 12½" x 70" (5) | - | - | 1 |
| 14" x 94" (6) | - | - | 1 |
| 6" x 85" (7) | - | - | 1 |
| 14" x 100" (8) | - | - | 1 |
| **Pieced Backing (optional)** | | | |
| 42" x 96" | - | - | 1 |
| 36" x 96" | - | - | 1 |
| 11" x 14" | - | - | 1 |
| 11" x 6" | - | - | 1 |

11"-wide strips of varying lengths, a total of approximately 105 inches long—fabrics A–C

**To make your own 1" binding:**

Cut and join 370" of 2"-wide strips (½ yard total fabric; I used the same fabric as my main backing [C]).

## Cutting

1. Using the Front Quilt Assembly Diagram as a guide, swatch or hold together fabrics you want to use and play with the arrangements until you find a combination of fabrics you like. I used a mix of chocolate brown, off-white, and purple for mine. To preserve the graphic simplicity of the design, choose a dark, a medium, and a light color.

2. Using the Cutting Key, cut and press the fabric for the quilt. Arrange the center squares and

# Assembly Diagrams

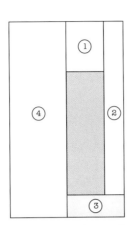

Block Assembly Diagram 1    Block Assembly Diagram 2

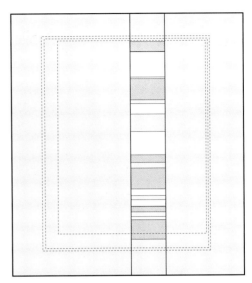

Back

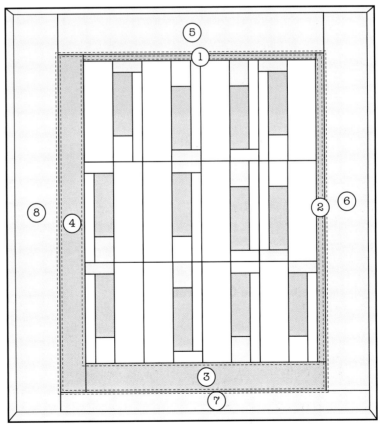

Front

logs on the design board according to the assembly diagrams for Blocks 1 and 2. You should have 5 versions of Block 1 and seven versions of Block 2.

## Building the Blocks

3.  Press the center squares and log strips. Piece all 12 blocks clockwise, sewing the first log for each block to the top edge of a center square, according to the Assembly Diagrams. Press the seams away from the center.

## Assembling the Quilt Front

4.  When you've completed all 12 blocks, press them neatly, and arrange them in 3 rows of 4 blocks each, rotating and distributing the 2 basic block designs to determine your favorite layout.

5.  Using the row joining technique on page 32, piece the blocks into 3 rows. Press the seam allowances in alternating directions. Join the rows together.

6.  Add "logs" around the 12-block patchwork quilt center. Starting at the top of your center square, pin and sew border strip 1 as your first log. Press the seam allowance away from the center. Continue adding the remaining border strips in a clockwise direction to complete the first and second tiers of the border.

## Assembling the Quilt Back

**7.** To piece the quilt back, lay out the 11"-wide fabric strips in a striped pattern. Start and finish the top and bottom of the column respectively with the 14"- and 6"-long strips using your main color, in my case chocolate brown (C). Piece the strips together into a 96"-long column.

**8.** Sew one of the remaining backing pieces to each side of the column, referring to the Back Assembly Diagram.

## Finishing the Quilt

**9.** Press the quilt top, muslin, and pieced backing. Make a quilt sandwich with your muslin (wrong side up), batting, and quilt top (right side up) only, and baste together, making sure that the layers are smooth and even.

**NOTE:** If you prefer to make a quilt without a pieced backing, use your backing fabric instead of the muslin to make the quilt sandwich and go to step 12.

**10.** This quilt uses quilting patterns at different stages of quilt assembly, including stitch-in-the-ditch quilting (which does not need to be marked). Begin to quilt around the largest log of each of the 12 blocks that forms the patchwork center. It's a good idea to match the thread in your bobbin to your muslin to ensure no dark color thread will peek through light fabric areas once the quilt is assembled.

**11.** To add your pieced quilt back, place the quilt back wrong side up on your work surface. Then place the quilt sandwich on top of the backing, muslin side facing down,. Smooth the layers and baste the quilt.

**12.** Now you're ready for additional quilting using the outline quilting technique (page 35). With a thread that matches the quilt back in your bobbin, begin quilting ¼" from the inner edge of the first border. Continue by quilting ¼" from the outer edge of the same border. Changing the needle thread color as necessary, quilt ¼" from the edge of the outer border.

**13.** Square up the quilt and baste around the perimeter edge. Bind the quilt to complete.

### DOUBLE YOUR QUILTS

I created an off-center patchwork stripe design for my quilt back. It's like making two quilts in one! To avoid stitching through my stripe pattern, I added a layer of muslin to my quilt sandwich. This extra layer allowed me to use stitch-in-the-ditch quilting on the pieced center of the front design. Then I added the pieced quilt back and outline quilting. Skip the muslin if you prefer a solid quilt back.

# ANNIVERSARY **QUILT**

**Difficulty:** 🧵🧵🧵🧵

**Type of block:** Picture Frame/
Color Story

**Techniques used:** column sashing (page 33), stitch-in-the-ditch quilting (page 35), binding (page 38), button embellishment (page 40)

Making a keepsake or memory quilt can be the perfect way to celebrate milestones and life events such as anniversaries and birthdays. I made my husband Andrew a quilt for our second (cotton) wedding anniversary, commemorating events and favorite places using photo transfers, Gocco prints, embroidery, and vintage button embellishments. Think of each log cabin block as a picture frame that shows off the special fabric or embellishment in the center square.

**Finished centers:** 5½″ x 5½″

**Finished logs:** 1″ wide (first and third tiers), 2″ wide (second tier)

**Finished block:** 15½″ x 15½″

**Number of blocks:** 25

**Binding:** about 330″ (9½ yards) of 1″ finished binding, handmade or purchased

**Finished quilt:** 80″ x 80″ (small full)

**You'll need:**

* 3 yards fabric for first and third tier logs and binding
* ¼ yard solid fabric for 5 embellished center squares
* If using photo transfer, you'll need ⅛ yard solid white fabric or four sheets of printable fabric. (Refer to recommendations from your photo transfer paper's manufacturer.) Makes 4 center squares.
* 2 yards of 108″-wide unbleached cotton muslin, or 5 yards of 44″-wide muslin or quilting cotton, for sashing and backing (B)
* 40–50 fabrics in assorted prints and patterns, in remnants or fat quarters (Cutting Key, Logs)
* Batting, at least 85″ x 85″ (I used Quilters Dream Cotton, which can be quilted up to 8″ apart)
* Off-white thread and thread to match first tier logs
* 1″ binding-tape maker (recommended)

For optional embellishments:
* Embroidery hoop, needle, and floss in colors of your choice
* Fabric marking pen
* Fabric printing supplies and fabric inks in colors of your choice
* Photo transfer supplies: Bubble Jet Set liquid, ⅛ yard white fabric, and freezer paper, *or* printable fabric sheets; ink-jet printer

| Cutting Key | A | B | Assorted |
|---|---|---|---|
| **Center Squares** | | | |
| 6" x 6" | - | - | 9 (solid fabrics for embellishment) |
| 6" x 6" | - | - | 16 (assorted prints) |
| **Logs** | | | |
| 1½" x 44" | 44 | - | - |
| 2½" x 40" | - | - | 25 (assorted prints) |

**NOTES:** You will use strips approximately 28" in total length for *each* first tier, 40" in total length for *each* second tier, and 50" in total length for *each* third tier of logs.

If making the pieced backing, cut the 2½"-wide logs to 44" in length and set aside leftover scraps to scrap-piece the backing stripes.

| **Sashing and Borders:** total of 948 inches of 2½"-wide strips | | | |
|---|---|---|---|
| 2½" x 108" (or 44") | - | 9 (or 22) | - |
| **Backing** | | | |
| 54" x 84" (pieced if necessary) | - | 1 | - |
| 2½" x 84" (pieced if necessary) | - | 1 | - |
| 24" x 84" (pieced if necessary) | - | 1 | - |

**To make your own 1" binding:**

Cut and join 330" of 2"-wide strips (½ yard total fabric; I used the same fabric as my first and third tiers of logs [A]).

## Cutting

1. Using the Block Assembly Diagram as a guide, swatch or hold together fabrics you want to use and play with the arrangements until you find a combination of fabrics you like. I used a solid fabric, blue for printing and white for photo transfer, and a mix of vintage and new prints in 4 color families (blue, green, pink, and brown) for the remaining center squares.

2. Using the Cutting Key, cut the fabric for the quilt. Use any printing techniques you like, such as photo transfer, to personalize the 9 solid-color center squares. Pair each center square with a complementary print to use in each block's second tier of logs.

## Building the Blocks

3. Chain-piece all 25 center squares to strips of fabric (A). Trim the logs and press. Then continue chain-piecing the joined center/log pieces to strips of fabric (A) to piece the remaining logs in this tier.

4. Build the second tier of each block individually, piecing all 4 logs from the fabric strip chosen

## Assembly Diagrams

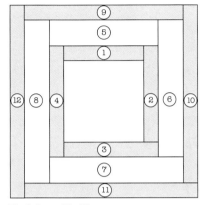

Block Assembly Diagram

Back

Front

for that block. Trim and press your blocks after each new log is added. Set all leftover strips of fabric aside.

5.  Repeat step 2 to chain-piece and press all 25 blocks to strips of fabric (A) to build the third tier.

6.  When you've completed all 25 blocks, press them neatly and add any additional embellishments, such as embroidery, if desired. (Refer to Making It Personal, below, for suggestions.)

## Assembling the Quilt Front

7.  Arrange the finished blocks on the design board in 5 rows of 5 blocks, moving the blocks around to determine your favorite layout. I chose to place blocks embellished with photo transfers at the center and at each side of the quilt, next to the blocks embellished using printing techniques, in a cross formation.

8.  Using the column sashing technique on page 33, join the first column of blocks together. Press. Join the second, third, fourth, and fifth the same way, pressing each column when you complete it.

9.  Now join your first and second columns with a vertical strip of sashing (pieced from shorter lengths if necessary), and repeat to join your second and third columns, third and fourth columns, and fourth and fifth columns. Press.

10. Using the adding borders technique on page 34, add the border strips to each side of the joined blocks to complete the quilt top, piecing if necessary. Press. It should now measure 80" square.

### MAKING IT PERSONAL

Use a combination of embellishments to personalize your quilt blocks. I chose to embroider my photo-transfer and printed center squares. For the photo blocks, I embroidered captions above and below the images, and stitched vintage buttons on, too. For my printed squares, I designed a simple map of Oregon, printed it in two colors, and embroidered our favorite places on each one, marking them with star buttons. Choose meaningful places or people to celebrate in your Anniversary Quilt, in whatever mediums you love best!

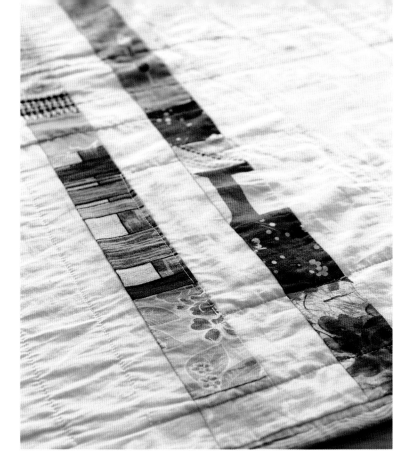

## Assembling the Quilt Back

**11.** Now it's time to piece the quilt's backing: two strips of patchwork prints on a muslin or quilting-cotton backing fabric. Using the fabric scraps you set aside in step 4, randomly scrap-piece the 2 strips in any order that appeals to you, using scraps of any length to make two 82"-long strips.

**12.** Pin and sew one patchwork strip to the 52" x 84" piece of backing fabric, right sides together. Then join the 2½"-wide backing fabric strip to the opposite edge of the patchwork strip. Join the remaining patchwork strip to the lower edge of the backing strip the same way. Join the remaining piece of backing fabric along the bottom edge of the second patchwork strip and press, ironing all seam allowances toward the patchwork strip center.

## Finishing the Quilt

**13.** Press the quilt top and pieced backing. Make a quilt sandwich with your pieced backing, batting, and quilt top, and baste together, making sure that the layers are smooth and even. You are ready to quilt!

**14.** This quilt uses stitch-in-the-ditch quilting (page 35), which does not need to be marked. Begin to quilt, stitching the outer seams of each of the first and third concentric tiers. To save time, you can work vertically and horizontally, lifting the presser foot up at the end of each log and repositioning at the next block, backstitching to begin and end each log. Stitch all 25 blocks individually or in this manner, trimming threads.

**15.** Square up the quilt and baste around the perimeter edge. Bind the quilt to complete.

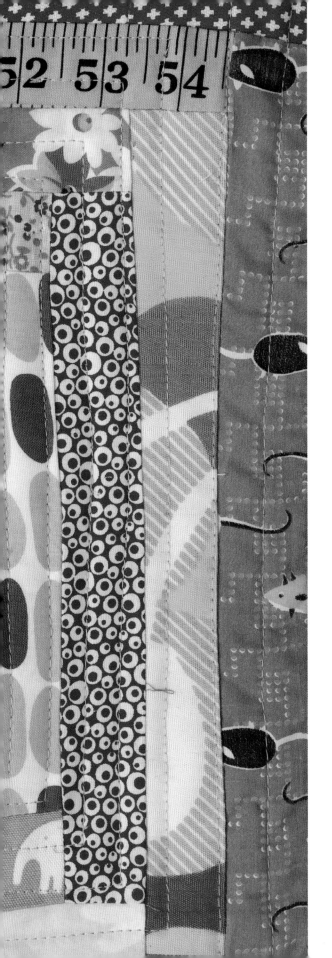

CHAPTER 4 HOME

\* DECOR \*

# FAVORITE CLOTH NAPKIN
# AND COASTER SET

**Difficulty:** 🧵🧵🧵🧵🧵

**Type of block:** Picture Frame

**Techniques used:** spotlighting centers (page 28), appliqué (page 40), double-fold hem (optional) (page 40)

It's easy to remember whose napkin and coaster are whose at a dinner party when a different log cabin motif is used for each set. Both projects are perfect for using up small scraps of fabric, and they're a very useful hostess or housewarming gift. Start with a purchased cloth napkin or sew your own, and back the simple reversible coaster with any patterned or solid fabric you like.

**NOTE:** These instructions are written for 1 napkin and coaster, but if you are making multiples at once, work in batches, cutting, piecing, and pressing all the blocks at the same time.

## FAVORITE CLOTH NAPKIN

**Finished center:** 2½" x 1½"

**Finished logs:** ¾" wide

**Finished block:** 3" x 4"

**Number of blocks:** 1

**Finished napkin:** 17" x 17"

**You'll need (for 1 napkin):**

* One cloth napkin
* 1 scrap of fabric for center square, at least 2" x 3" (A)
* Scraps of fabric for logs (B)
* 2" x 3" piece of pattern paper, for spotlighting center

**NOTE:** You can make your own cloth napkins for this project from one fat quarter of fabric for each napkin. Cut the fabric to 18" x 18" (or the size you'd like) and stitch a simple double-fold hem all around the perimeter to finish.

## Assembly Diagrams

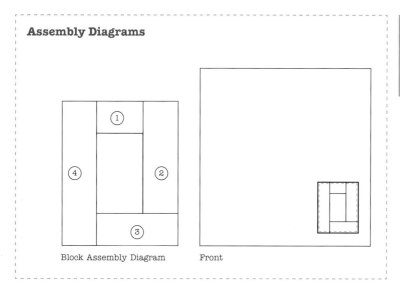

Block Assembly Diagram     Front

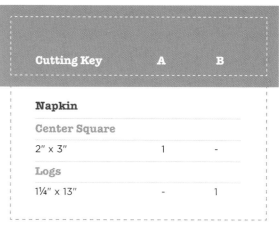

| Cutting Key | A | B |
|---|---|---|
| **Napkin** | | |
| Center Square | | |
| 2" x 3" | 1 | - |
| Logs | | |
| 1¼" x 13" | - | 1 |

## Cutting

1. Using the Block Assembly Diagram as a guide, swatch or hold together fabrics you want to use and play with the arrangements until you find a combination of fabrics you like. I used assorted browns and tans with a botanical theme.

2. Using the Cutting Key, cut and press the fabric for the napkin. Use the pattern paper and the spotlighting centers technique to cut the center square. I spotlighted a graphic leaf pattern for my center square.

## Building the Block

3. Using the log strip and center square, build the one-tier napkin block according to the Napkin Block Assembly Diagram, beginning with log 1. Press the finished block.

## Assembling the Napkin

4. Using the appliqué technique on page 40, press ¼" to the wrong side of the block along each edge. Clip the corners if necessary. Pin the block to the napkin cloth in the lower right corner, about 1" in from both edges or in the location of your choice.

5. Stitch the block to the napkin a scant ⅛" seam allowance from the folded-under edge, back-stitching at the beginning and end to hold the seam. Press.

# ROUNDABOUT COASTERS

**Difficulty:**

**Type of block:** Picture Frame

**Techniques used:** spotlighting centers (page 28), stitch-in-the-ditch quilting (page 35), binding (page 38)

**Finished center:** 1½" x 2½"

**Finished logs:** ¾" wide (logs 1 and 3); 1¼" wide (logs 2 and 4)

**Finished block:** 5" x 5"

**Number of blocks:** 1

**Binding:** about 22" (¾ yard) of ¾" binding, handmade or purchased

**Finished coaster:** 5" x 5"

## You'll need (for 1 coaster):

* ⅛ yard fabric for center and binding (this is enough for several coasters) (A)
* Scraps of fabric for logs (B)
* 5½" x 5½" piece of batting
* 5½" x 5½" piece of fabric for backing (C)
* ¾" binding-tape maker (recommended)

## Cutting

1. Following steps 1 and 2 of the Favorite Cloth Napkin project and referring to the Coaster Cutting Key, choose, cut, and press your fabric for the coaster.

## Building the Block

2. Build the one-tier coaster block according to the Coaster Block Assembly Diagram, beginning with log 1. Piece the narrow strips to the short sides of the center square and the wide strips to the long sides. Press the block.

## Assembly Diagrams

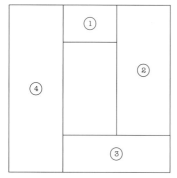

Block Assembly Diagram

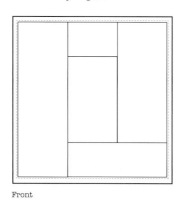

Front

| Cutting Key | A | B | C |
| --- | --- | --- | --- |
| **Coaster** | | | |
| Center Square | | | |
| 2" x 3" | 1 | - | - |
| Logs | | | |
| 1¼" x 6" (1 and 3) | - | 1 | - |
| 1¾" x 10" (2 and 4) | - | 1 | - |
| Backing | | | |
| 5½" x 5½" | - | - | 1 |

**To make your own ¾" binding:**

Cut a 22" strip of 1½"-wide fabric (I used the same fabric as my center square [A]).

## Finishing the Coaster

3. Make a quilt sandwich with your backing fabric, batting, and pieced coaster top and baste together, making sure the layers are smooth and even. You are ready to quilt!

4. Stitch in the ditch around the center rectangle (or quilt as desired). Square up the coaster.

5. Bind the coaster as you would a quilt, stitching securely all around the coaster and turning corners as usual. As you approach the final corner, stop sewing ¼" from the corner. Because the sides are so short, layer the unfinished binding ends on top of one another. Trim the binding tail so it overlaps the first binding edge by at least 2" and fold under the end. Press.

6. Then create your folded corner the same way you normally would, pinning or hand-basting the last section down for your final machine-stitching. (I like to hand-baste this last couple of inches the same way I do at corners.) Backstitch at the beginning and end of the stitching to sew the final section of your binding.

# CHEERFUL POT HOLDERS

**Difficulty:** 🧵🧵

**Type of block:** Color Story

**Techniques used:** spotlighting centers (page 28), diagonal quilting (page 35), binding (page 38)

Make these simple, bright pot holders with favorite prints or colorful scraps from other projects. They're quick to piece and easy to quilt in a crosshatch pattern. A border of handmade binding with a handy loop for hanging is just the thing to finish them up!

**Finished center:** 1½" x 1½"

**Finished logs:** 1" wide

**Finished block size:** 8½" x 8½"

**Number of blocks:** 1

**Binding:** about 45" (1¼ yards) of 1" binding, handmade or purchased

**Finished pot holder:** 8½" x 8½"

## You'll need (for 1 pot holder):

* ¼ yard fabric for centers, logs, and backing (A)
* Scraps of 4 other fabrics for logs (B–E)
* 45" purchased 1" binding or ⅛ yard fabric for binding and 1" binding-tape maker, if making your own (F)
* 10" x 10" piece of batting
* 10" x 10" piece of heat-resistant batting such as Insul-Bright
* 2" x 2" piece of pattern paper

| Cutting Key | A | Assorted |
|---|---|---|
| **Center Square** | | |
| 2" x 2" | 1 | - |
| **Logs** | | |
| 1½" x 10" (1 and 7) | - | 1 |
| 1½" x 10" (2 and 8) | - | 1 |
| 1½" x 10" (3 and 5) | - | 1 |
| 1½" x 10" (4 and 6) | - | 1 |
| 1½" x 30" | 1 | - |
| **Backing** | | |
| 8¾" x 8¾" | — | 1 |
| **To make your own 1" binding:** | | |
| Cut a 45"-long, 2"-wide strip of fabric. | | |

## Cutting

1. Using the Block Assembly Diagram as a guide, swatch or hold together fabrics you want to use and play with the arrangements until you find a combination of fabrics you like. Choose a main fabric (A) and 4 other scraps of assorted fabrics that complement it in a color story of your choice. I made 2 pot holders, one that mixed assorted greens in with the main fabric and one that mixed in assorted yellows and oranges. I scrap-pieced one of my green logs together from two fabrics I liked.

2. Using the Cutting Key, cut and press the fabric for the pot holder. Use the pattern paper and the spotlighting centers technique to cut the center square. I spotlighted a cookbook image from the design printed on my fabric.

## Building the Block

3. Build the 3-tier block according to the Block Assembly Diagram, beginning with log 1. In tiers 1 and 2, logs made from the same fabric should face each other in different tiers across the design. Tier 3 should be pieced all from the same fabric (E). Press the block neatly.

## Finishing the Pot Holder

4. Now you'll mark your pot holder for quilting. This pot holder uses a two-direction diagonal quilting pattern (page 35). Using a quilting ruler and washable fabric marker, mark diagonal quilting lines at a 45-degree angle to the sides of your center square, from upper left to bottom right for a total of 4 diagonal lines in each direction.

**Assembly Diagrams**

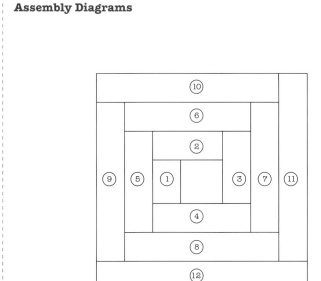

Block Assembly Diagram

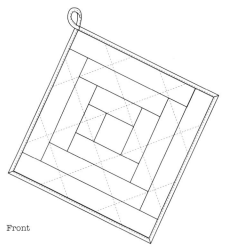

Front

5.  Make a quilt sandwich with your backing fabric, batting, heat-resistant batting, and finished pot holder top and baste them together, making sure all layers are smooth and even. You are ready to quilt!

6.  With a thread color that complements your fabric, begin to quilt the crosshatch lines from corner to corner, sewing the lines that meet the corners of the center square first. Then quilt the sections closer to the corners. Square up the pot holder and stitch around the perimeter.

7.  Bind the pot holder as you would a quilt, starting at the edge of the upper left corner and stitching securely all around the pot holder, turning corners as usual. When you reach the final corner, do not turn. Instead, catch the first raw edge of binding inside the binding tail, and continue stitching to the end of the tail, sewing its folded halves closed. This sealed length of binding will become the pot holder's loop.

8.  Trim the extra binding tail to 6" and turn under the end ¼", pressing it firmly. Pin the binding tail to the corner of the pot holder in a neat loop, pinning the folded section down at the corner. Stitch the loop neatly into place, backstitching at the beginning and end of the stitching.

Cheerful Pot Holders

# COLOR BLOCK **TEA TOWELS**

**Difficulty:** 🧵🧵

**Type of block:** Picture Frame

**Techniques used:** diagonal quilting (page 35), binding (page 38), double-fold hem (page 40), appliqué (page 40)

This graphic-contrast appliqué project joins three pieces of fabric to make the "center square" in this log cabin design—a simple and striking elongated rectangle. I started with side-hemmed linen tea towel fabric sold by the yard, but you can use fabric you have or a plain premade tea towel for this project, too. Handmade binding to match the logs is a nice finishing touch.

**Finished center:** 2½" x 15" pieced horizontal rectangle

**Finished Logs:** 1" wide

**Finished block:** 4½" x 17"

**Number of blocks:** 1

**Binding:** about 36" (1 yard) of ¾" binding, handmade or purchased

**Finished tea towel:** 17" x 24"

**NOTE:** These directions are based on a 17"-wide tea towel. The log cabin appliqué covers it from side to side. If your towel is a different width, you'll need to make adjustments for the size. Consider a smaller, centered applique if you want to eliminate the math!

### You'll need (for 1 towel):

* ⅔ yard fabric for towel (C), or a premade tea towel
* ⅛ yard fabric for center squares (A)
* ⅛ yard fabric for logs and binding (B)
* ¾" binding tape maker (recommended)
* Fabric dye (optional)

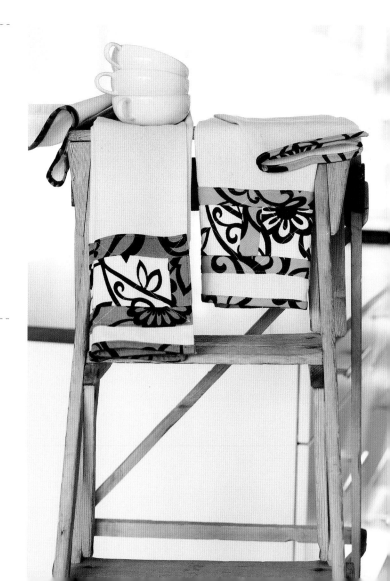

| Cutting Key (for 1 towel) | A | B | C |
|---|---|---|---|
| **Towels** | | | |
| 19" x 24" | - | - | 1 |
| **Center Squares** | | | |
| 3" x 7½" | 2 | - | - |
| **Logs** | | | |
| 1½" x 44" | - | 1 | - |
| 1½" x 3" | - | 1 | - |

**To make your own ¾" binding** (to hem top and bottom edges of towel):
Cut a 36"-long, 1½"-wide strip of fabric (B) to yield two 18" lengths of ¾"
finished binding.

**NOTE:** Adjust the cutting key as follows to use a towel of another size.
Width of center squares: (Width of finished towel minus 2") divided by 2
Total inches needed of log fabric: Finished binding length plus 9"
Total length of binding: (Width of towel plus 1") times 2

## Cutting

1. Using the Block Assembly Diagram as a guide, swatch or hold together fabrics you want to use
   and play with the arrangements until you find a combination of fabrics you like. I chose to hand-
   dye a white patterned fabric (A) to create both an olive green and an aqua fabric for the logs
   (B) that contrasted nicely with the original white. Fabric dye is an easy and inexpensive way to
   dramatically change the look of a fabric.

2. Using the Cutting Key, cut and press the fabric. Set the center squares and logs aside.

## Making the Towel

**NOTE:** If using a premade towel, skip ahead to step 5.

3. Using a ½" seam allowance and the double-fold hem technique on page 40, hem each long
   edge of the towel fabric. Leave the short edges unfinished.

4. Using the binding technique on page 38, make and attach your finished binding to the top
   and bottom edges of your towel. Press the binding ends under ¼", trimming the fold if bulky.
   Now pin one length of the binding tape to each end of the towel. Stitch the binding down, backstitching at each end to hold the stitching securely. The binding creates a neat finish for
   the towel.

Color Block Tea Towels

## Assembly Diagrams

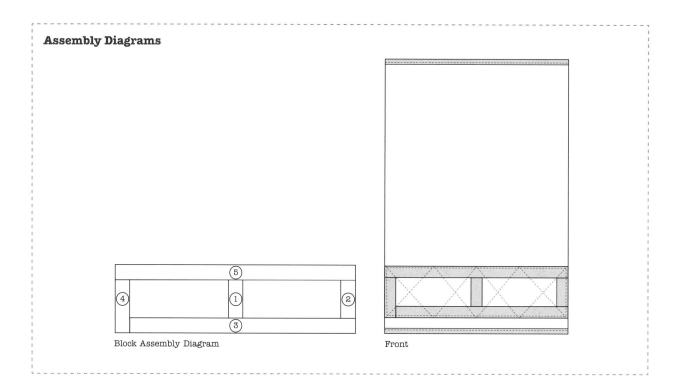

Block Assembly Diagram

Front

### Building the Block

**5.** Following the Block Assembly Diagram, piece a 3"-long log 1 between 2 center squares to make 1 long center rectangle, around which you'll build a block.

**6.** Build the one-tier block according to the Block Assembly Diagram, beginning with log 2. Press ¼" to the wrong side of the block along each unfinished edge, and trim the corners if bulky. Using the appliqué technique on page 40, pin the block to the tea towel 1" above one bound edge, and stitch in place.

### Finishing the Towel

**7.** Now you'll mark your block for quilting. This tea towel uses a two-direction diagonal quilting pattern (page 35). Using 5 pins each at the top and bottom edges of the blocks, mark the corners, the center points, and the points halfway between the corners and centers. You are ready to quilt!

**NOTE:** You can also mark these diagonal quilting lines with a quilting ruler and washable marker, but I liked the softer look of a relaxed quilt line for my towels, so I simply used pins as guide points for a freehand crosshatch quilting design.

**8.** With white thread, begin to quilt the diagonal lines from the bottom left corner, stitching diagonal lines and pivoting at each pin. Finish by backstitching to secure the quilting.

# POLKA-DOT **PINCUSHION**

**Difficulty:** 🧵🧵

**Type of block:** Picture Frames

**Techniques used:** button embellishment (page 40)

This simple little pincushion (with a tiny needle sharpener attached) is perfect for using favorite scraps or fat quarters. I chose two micro-polka-dot prints in contrasting colors from the same fabric collection, but you can pair any combination you like of solids, prints, or a mix of both—polka dots or not. Tuft the cushion with an oversized button, a design detail echoed on the smaller sharpener cushion, too!

**Finished center:** ½" x ½"

**Finished logs:** ½" wide

**Finished block:** 5" x 5" (pincushion); 1½" x 1½" (needle-sharpener)

**Number of blocks:** 2

**Finished size:** 5" x 5" pincushion with 1½" x 1½" needle sharpener

## You'll need:
* ¼ yard each of 2 coordinating fabrics (A and B)
* A handful of polyfil stuffing
* Superfine steel wool (you can find this at any hardware store)
* ⅛" satin ribbon, at least 5" long
* Hand-sewing needle
* Thread (I used black for machine-sewing and attaching buttons, and invisible threads for hand-sewing)
* 2 shank buttons, 1 large and 1 small (mine measured about 1¼" and ⅜" across)
* 2 flat buttons, 1 medium/large and 1 small (mine measured about 1" and ⅜" across)

| Cutting Key | A | B |
| --- | --- | --- |
| **Center Squares** | | |
| 1" x 1" | 1 | - |
| 1" x 1" | - | 1 |
| **Logs** | | |
| 1" x 45" | 1 | - |
| 1" x 25" | - | 1 |
| **Backing** | | |
| 5½" x 5½" | - | 1 |
| 2" x 2" | - | 1 |

## Cutting

1. Using the Block Assembly Diagram as a guide, swatch or hold together fabrics you want to use and play with the arrangements until you find a combination of fabrics you like. I used 2 versions of exactly the same prints, in opposite colorways (black fabric with light aqua polka dots and a light aqua fabric with black polka dots), but any 2 harmonizing fabrics would be nice for this simple Picture Frames pattern.

2. Using the Cutting Key, cut and press the fabric for the pincushion and needle sharpener.

## Building the Blocks

3. Using the fabric (A) center square, build the 4-tier pincushion block according to the Block Assembly Diagram. Beginning with log 1, piece the first tier, then alternate the fabrics with each subsequent tier, (B), (A), (B), (A), for a concentric-squares effect. Press the block neatly.

4. Pin and sew the pincushion top and backing, right sides together, using a ¼" seam allowance, leaving a 2½" opening along one edge for turning .

5. Using the fabric (B) center square, build the one-tier needle-sharpener block according to the Block Assembly Diagram. Beginning with log 1, piece each log using fabric (A). Press the block neatly.

6. Pin and sew 3 sides of the needle-sharpener top and backing, right sides together, using a ¼" seam allowance. Leave one side open for turning.

## Finishing the Pincushion

7. Turn both cushions right side out, making sure the corners are sharp and neat. Press. Stuff the pincushion with polyfil and the needle sharpener with steel wool. Pin each opening closed and mark the center of the opening.

8. Begin securely hand-stitching the pincushion opening closed with invisible thread. Stop sewing just before the center mark. Insert the ribbon, slipping an unfinished end inside the opening, and continue stitching until the opening is closed and the ribbon is secured. You may want to add a bit more polyfil just before finishing the stitching. Your cushion should be nice and plump.

9. Stitch the needle sharpener closed in the same way, securing the remaining unfinished end of the ribbon at the center mark. The steel wool will be fairly compact and not as lofty as the polyfil; don't overstuff the cushion, just make sure it's evenly filled.

10. Thread your hand-sewing needle with coordinating thread, and bring it up through the center square of the pincushion, from the bottom to the top, and leave the knot dangling. Bring the needle through the shank of the first large button and then bring it back down through the cushion very close to the first stitch. Slip the needle through the dangling knotted thread tail to catch and gently tug the thread until it is taut and the button is indented in the top of the cushion.

11. Add the medium-sized flat button to the bottom of the pincushion, covering that first stitch, and continue passing the needle up through the shank button on the top and then down through the sew-through button on the bottom to tuft the cushion. After 6 or 7 stitches, knot securely on the bottom of the cushion, under the flat button.

12. Follow steps 10 and 11 to tuft the needle sharpener in the same manner, using the small shank button on top and the small flat button on the bottom.

**Assembly Diagrams**

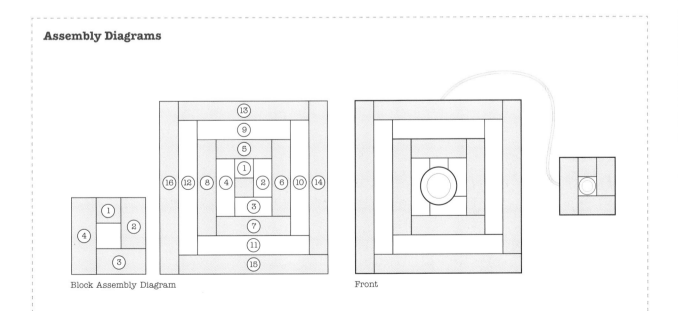

Block Assembly Diagram

Front

# BLOCK POCKET **APRON**

**Difficulty:** 🧵🧵🧵

**Type of block:** Picture Frame

**Techniques used:** spotlighting centers (page 28), binding (modern version only) (page 38), double-fold hem (page 40), patch pocket (page 41)

Make yourself (or a friend) a pretty apron with a self-lined quilt block pocket. The secret to this project is converting an already-hemmed pillowcase into the body of the apron. Then add purchased extra-wide bias or binding tape for the sash. You can make a streamlined, modern version or a sweetly detailed and gathered vintage version; it's up to you (and your pillowcase!).

**Finished center:** 4" x 3"

**Finished logs:** 1" wide

**Finished block:** 8" x 7½" (Modern); 8" x 7" (Vintage)

**Number of blocks:** 1

**Binding:** about 9" (¼ yard) of ¾" binding, handmade or purchased (Modern only)

**Finished pocket:** 8" x 7½" (Modern) or 8" x 7" (Vintage)

**You'll need:**
* 1 standard pillowcase
* Scraps of 2 coordinating fabrics for the block pocket, (A) and (B)
* 2½ yards purchased 2" (extra-wide) binding tape
* 4" x 3" piece of pattern paper
* Thread that matches your pillowcase, binding, and fabric (B)

For the Modern version only:
* 9" x 1½" strip of fabric for binding and ¾" finished binding-tape maker, if making your own (B)

| Cutting Key | A | B |
|---|---|---|
| **Apron Body, choose 1 (see project instructions)** | | |
| MODERN: 20″ x 30″, cut from pillowcase (1) | | |
| OR | | |
| VINTAGE: 17″ x 32″, cut from pillowcase (1) | | |
| **Pocket** | | |
| **Center Square** | | |
| 4½″ x 3½″ | 1 | - |
| **Logs** | | |
| 1½″ x 18″ | - | 1 |
| 1½″ x 30″ | 1 | - |
| **To make your own ¾″ binding** (Modern version only): | | |
| Cut a 9″-long, 1½″-wide strip of fabric (B). | | |

## Cutting

1. Choose a pillowcase to turn into your apron, and then select 2 fabrics for the pocket. For my Modern Apron I chose a plain light green case and 2 bright prints; for my Vintage Apron I chose a white case embellished with cross-stitch to complement a vintage tea-towel calendar and cheerful floral print.

2. Using the Cutting Key for the Modern or the Vintage version, cut the fabric for the apron. Use the pattern paper and the spotlighting centers technique to cut out the center square.

## Building the Block

3. Build the 2-tier block according to the Block Assembly Diagram, beginning with log 1. Press the block neatly.

## Make the Apron

4. Press your pillowcase and cut the top (folded) seam away, as shown on the diagram. Note any design you'd like to feature (like the cross-stitch on my vintage pillowcase) and fold the case lengthwise to center. This will become the front of your apron. Mark the back side of the case exactly opposite the center front design. Make a neat cut all the way up the back, to yield a large, flat piece of fabric. If there is no design to center, as in the Modern pillowcase, simply cut along a seam.

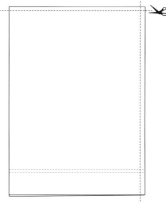

Cutting the pillow case

**5.** Measure and mark the following distance from the bottom (hemmed) edge of the pillowcase: 20″ for the Modern Apron and 17″ for the Vintage Apron, or the apron length as desired. Cut away any excess fabric above that line and set aside. This will be your waistband edge. Then cut away any extra width, as you like. I also cut off 4″ on each side of the case to make a more compact apron shape, as described in the Cutting Key.

**6.** Using the double-fold hem technique on page 40, hem each side edge of the apron ½″ and press. Leave the top, waistband edge unfinished. For reference, my Modern Apron measured 28″ x 20″, and my Vintage Apron measured 30″ x 17″.

## Assembling the Block Pocket

**7.** Using the fabric set aside in step 5, cut a piece of backing fabric the same size as your pieced block. Using a ¼″ seam allowance, pin and stitch together the backing and block, right sides together, on 3 sides, leaving the top edge of your pocket open. Clip the corners and turn right side out. This is the lined pocket.

**8.** Finish the pocket edges: For the Modern block pocket use the binding technique on page 38 to make and attach your finished binding to the top edge of the pocket so that 1″ of binding extends past each side. Press the binding ends under, trimming the fold if bulky. Stitch the binding down, back-stitching at each end to hold the seam securely. For the Vintage block pocket, fold in and press the top, unfinished edges ¼″. Pin and sew using a scant ⅛″ from the edge.

## Finishing the Apron

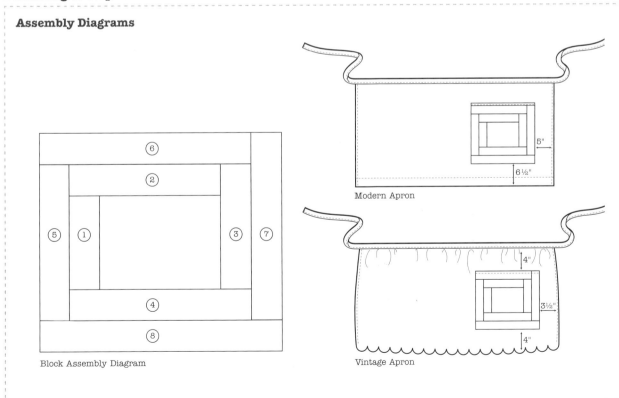

**Assembly Diagrams**

Block Assembly Diagram

Modern Apron

Vintage Apron

9.  Neatly press the pocket and its corners. Pin the pocket to the apron as desired. I centered my Modern pocket vertically, 5" from the left side of the apron; and I placed my Vintage pocket 3½" from the left and 4" from the bottom sides of the apron, 4" from the waistband edge.

11. Using the patch pockets technique on page 41, stitch your pocket onto the apron. You are ready to add the sash to the waistband!

12. Cut both ends of the extra-wide binding at a slight angle. Fold under and press the unfinished edges. Edgestitch from one angled end along the fold to the other angled end. This will add stability to your apron's sash. Do not stitch the open edge of the binding closed.

13. Attach the sash: For the Modern version, mark the center of your binding sash and the center of your apron waist. Pin the open bottom of your binding sash over the unfinished edge of the apron top, aligning the centers. Edgestitch the entire length of the binding, catching the apron in the waistband.

    For the Vintage version, use a long basting stitch to baste ¼" in along the waistband edge of the apron. Leave long thread tails at the beginning and the end. Gently pull the thread tails to gather the edge for a soft ruffled effect. (After gathering, my apron measured about 22" wide at the waistband edge and 30" at the bottom.) Reset your machine stitch length to its normal setting, then pin and stitch the sash to the apron as for the Modern version.

## MAKING IT PERSONAL

If you have a favorite pillowcase that's missing its mate, this is a lovely way to give it new life. Choose a special fabric for the pocket's center square if you like. (I cut my birthday month out of a vintage Vera tea towel calendar for my Vintage version of the apron.) And if it's a gift, choose a pillowcase and pocket fabrics that remind you of the recipient! You could also use the oversized center square as an embroidery or printing palette, or add buttons or trims to embellish the pocket. You could even coordinate your fabric choices with a set of matching Cheerful Pot Holders (page 107) for a thoughtful holiday gift or housewarming present.

# COLOR STORY **PILLOW**

**Difficulty:** 🧵🧵

**Type of block:** Color Story

**Techniques used:** spotlighting centers (page 28), stitch-in-the-ditch quilting (page 35), geometric quilting (page 35), double-fold hem (page 40), envelope pillow back (page 41)

This colorful pillow mixes prints in four different color families to draw the eye all around the block. I used a handful of cheerful fabrics in red (the star of the "story" here), light blue, yellow, and gray, arranging them to make up six tiers of logs, and quilted the pillow front with an ultra-simple, geometric, boxy spiral to echo the piecing.

**Finished center:** 1½"

**Finished logs:** 1" wide

**Finished block:** 14½"

**Number of blocks:** 1

**Finished pillow:** 14" x 14"

**You'll need:**

* ⅛ yard each of fabrics in 4 color families—I used red, pale blue, yellow, and gray (A–D)
* 16" x 16" piece of batting
* 16" x 16" piece of solid fabric for interior (hidden) backing
* ⅓ yard fabric for the pillow's envelope back (A), plus scrap for center square
* 14" x 14" pillow form
* 2" x 2" piece of pattern paper
* Light gray thread

| Cutting Key | Assorted Red | Assorted Blue | Assorted Yellow | Assorted Gray |
|---|---|---|---|---|
| **Center Square** | | | | |
| 2" x 2" | 1 | - | - | - |
| **Logs** | | | | |
| 1½" x 15" | - | 6 | - | - |
| 1½" x 15" | - | - | 6 | - |
| 1½" x 15" | 6 | - | - | - |
| 1½" x 15" | - | - | - | 6 |

**NOTE:** The longest strip needed for this block is 15" long, and for freedom of design, I like to start with each log strip cut at 15". However, you can cut some strips shorter. The shortest strip needed (log 1) to build this block is 2" long.

| | | | | |
|---|---|---|---|---|
| **Envelope Pillow Back** | | | | |
| 13" x 15" | 2 | - | - | - |

## Cutting

1. Using the Block Assembly Diagram as a guide, swatch or hold together fabrics in 4 different color families you want to use and play with the arrangements until you find a combination of fabrics you like. You can use as many prints within each color family as you want.

2. Using the Cutting Key, cut and press the fabric for the pillow. Use the pattern paper and the spotlighting centers technique to cut the center square, keeping in mind that the final size will be 1½" x 1½". I chose to spotlight a pair of scissors (A).

## Building the Block

3. Build the 6-tier block according to the Block Assembly Diagram, beginning with log 1. Use fabric (B) for logs 1, 3, 10, 12, 17, and 19; fabric (C) for logs 2, 4, 9, 11, 18, and 20; fabric (A) for logs 5, 7, 14, 16, 21, and 23; and fabric (D) for logs 6, 8, 13, 15, 22, and 24. Press the block after piecing each tier. Your finished block should measure 14½" x 14½".

**NOTE:** I intentionally repeated several fabrics within the color-story pattern. If you'd like to follow my pillow design, repeat prints within each color family as follows: 1 print from fabric (B) in logs 3 and 10, from fabric (C) in logs 9 and 18, and from fabric (D) in logs 15 and 24. Repeat 2 prints from fabric (A), in the center square and log 22 and another print in logs 5 and 16.

## Finishing the Pillow

6. Now you'll mark your pillow top for quilting. This pillow uses stitch-in-the-ditch (which you do not need to mark) and geometric quilting. With a quilting ruler and washable marker, mark squares ⅓"–½" from the center square to form an expanding squared spiral pattern, or plan to

quilt the squares freehand, as I did. If you mark your lines, you'll have 2 quilting lines on each log; I used 14 expanding squares, each building off the last, to reach the edge of the pillow top.

7. Make a quilt sandwich with your backing fabric, batting, and finished pillow top and baste them together, making sure all layers are smooth and even. You are ready to quilt!

8. With light gray thread, begin to quilt by first stitching in the ditch around the perimeter of the center square. Then, quilt the geometric quilting lines, beginning at the center of the pillow top and working toward the edges. Square up your pillow top.

9. Following the envelope pillow back technique on page 41, make a 1" double-fold hem (page 40) along one long (15") edge of each piece of pillow back fabric. Continue following the envelope pillow back technique to join the envelope closure to the pillow top, right sides together, using a ¼" seam allowance.

10. Clip the corners if necessary. Turn the cover right side out and press. Insert a 14" x 14" pillow form.

## Assembly Diagrams

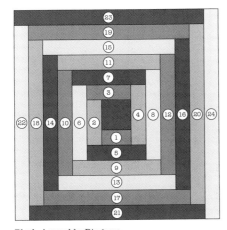

Block Assembly Diagram

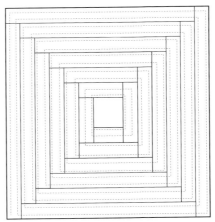

Front

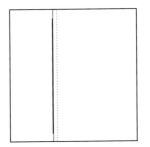

Back

# RECYCLED CORDS **PILLOW**

**Difficulty:** 🧵🧵

**Type of block:** Picture Frame, Color Story

**Techniques used:** spotlighting centers (page 28), geometric quilting (page 35), stitch-in-the-ditch quilting (page 35), double-fold hem (page 40), envelope pillow back (page 41)

This is the first log cabin project I ever made, and it is still one of my favorites! Pillows are great projects for beginners, and I think starting with a Picture Frames style can be especially useful. You can experiment with mixing prints together while using solid "frames" to keep the design orderly. Reuse corduroy from an old pair of pants (or any other neutral fabric) to frame and separate brighter tiers of prints in a few favorite colors. Best of all, a single block becomes a useful household necessity—you can never have too many cute pillows!

**Finished center:** 3½" x 3½"

**Finished logs:** 1" wide (logs 1 and 3); 2" wide (logs 2 and 4)

**Finished block:** 15½" x 15½"

**Number of blocks:** 1

**Finished pillow:** 15" x 15"

### You'll need (for 1 pillow):
* 1 scrap of fabric for center square, at least 4" x 4" (A)
* 1 pair of corduroy pants, or ⅛ yard of neutral fabric (B)
* 8 assorted fabric scraps
* 17" x 17" piece of batting
* 17" x 17" piece of solid fabric for interior (hidden) backing
* ⅓ yard fabric for the pillow's envelope back (C)
* 14" x 14" pillow form
* 4" x 4" piece of pattern paper

| Cutting Key | A | B | C | Assorted |
|---|---|---|---|---|
| **Center Square** | | | | |
| 4" x 4" | 1 | - | - | - |
| **Logs** | | | | |
| 2½" x 16" | - | - | - | 8 |
| 1½" x 60" total, (pieced if necessary) | - | 1 | - | - |

**NOTES:** The longest strip needed for this block is 16" long, and for freedom of design, I like to start with each log strip cut at 16". However, you can cut some strips shorter. The shortest strip needed (log 1) to build this block is 6" long.

When cutting fabric (B) into strips, the length of each one will depend on the size and shape of the reclaimed garment. Scrap-piece strips together to get the length you need for each log. This project uses 60" total of fabric (B).

| | | | | |
|---|---|---|---|---|
| **Envelope Pillow Back** | | | | |
| 12" x 16" | - | - | 2 | - |

## Cutting

1. Using the Block Assembly Diagram as a guide, swatch or hold together fabrics you want to use and play with the arrangements until you find a combination of fabrics you like. Choose a mix of 8 patterned fabrics you enjoy together for the logs; they don't have to "match," but their colors should relate nicely and coordinate with your center-square fabric and corduroy. I made 2 pillows, one that paired oranges and browns with brown corduroy and one that mixed in yellows and blues with tan corduroy.

2. Using the Cutting Key, cut and press the fabric for the pillow. Use the pattern paper and the spotlighting centers technique to cut the center square. I chose one of Denyse Schmidt's prints for my center square. Place the center square and the logs on the design board, moving the log fabrics around until you like the mix.

## Building the Block

3. Build the 4-tier block according to the Block Assembly Diagram. Beginning with log 1, piece the first tier, then alternate the fabrics with each subsequent tier, (B), (assorted), (B), (assorted). Press the block neatly. The pieced block should measure 16" square.

## Finishing the Pillow

4. Press the pillow top. You are ready to mark your pillow top for quilting. This pillow uses geometric quilting and stitch-in-the-ditch quilting (which does not need to be marked). I quilted horizontally, ½"–¾" apart, without marking my lines. Do not extend the quilting lines through the center square—leaving it unquilted will help it "pop" in the design.

**NOTE:** You can also mark these quilting lines with a quilting ruler and washable marker, but I liked the softer look of a relaxed quilt line for my pillow.

5. Make a quilt sandwich with the backing fabric, batting, and pillow top, and baste them together, making sure that the layers are smooth and even. You are ready to quilt!

6. Begin to quilt the horizontal lines in a thread color that complements your overall design, from left to right all over the block. Then, stitch in the ditch around the center square, backstitching at the beginning and ending of each quilting line. Square up your pillow top.

7. Following the envelope pillow back technique on page 41, make a ½" double-fold hem (page 40) along one long (16") edge of each piece of pillow back fabric. I used a decorative zigzag stitch to sew the hem. Continue following the envelope pillow back technique to join the envelope closure to the pillow top, right sides together, using a ¼" seam allowance.

8. Clip the corners if necessary. Turn the cover right side out and press. Insert a 14" x 14" pillow form.

**Assembly Diagrams**

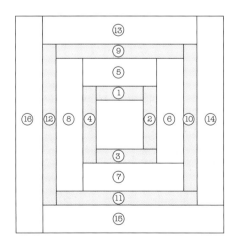

Block Assembly Diagram

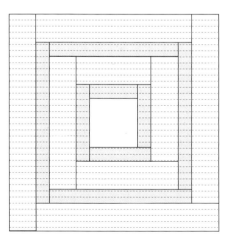

Front

Back

# STARRY NIGHT **PILLOW**

**Difficulty:** 🧵🧵

Type of block: Picture Frames

**Techniques used:** chain-piecing (page 31), column joining (page 32), adding borders (page 34), stitch-in-the-ditch quilting (page 35), double-fold hem (page 40), envelope pillow back (page 41)

Small patchwork projects like pillows are perfect for experimenting with new types of fabric or new color combinations. My friend and technical editor Sue Kopp inspired this design—her beautiful quilting with sizzling, striking batiks led me to try my luck with them for the first time. I fell in love with a deep blue batik patterned with organic drips and splashes and paired it with a hot and fiery yellow that popped against it. Once I chose my fabrics, they told me exactly what to do next: mix tiny, bold centers into a serene two-tier block, like stars punctuating a night sky. Sixteen blocks later, I had a new favorite pillow.

**Finished center:** ½" x ½"

**Finished logs:** ½" wide

**Finished block:** 3" x 3"

**Number of blocks:** 16

**Finished pillow:** 12½" x 12½"

**You'll need:**

* ¾ yard dark blue batik for logs and envelope back (B)
* ⅛ yard yellow batik for center squares (A)
* 14" x 14" piece of batting
* 14" x 14" piece of solid fabric for the interior (hidden) backing
* 12" x 12" pillow form
* Thread (I used dark blue)

| Cutting Key | A | B |
|---|---|---|
| **Center Square Strips** | | |
| 1" x 8½" | 2 | - |
| **Logs and Borders** | | |
| 1" x 44" | - | 10 |
| **NOTE:** Your center strips will be cut down to 1" x 1" squares after you join them to the first log strip. | | |
| **Envelope Pillow Back** | | |
| 13" x 13" | - | 2 |

## Cutting

1. Using the Cutting Key, cut the fabric for your pillow. As noted in the Key, cut the center square fabric (A) into 2 strips.

## Building the Blocks

2. Align and sew the long edges of a blue strip of fabric (B) with a yellow strip (A), right sides together, using a standard ¼" seam allowance. Using a quilting ruler and rotary cutter, trim the ends of the strips, and then cut this first joined strip into 8 joined 1" center square/first log pieces. Press.

3. Chain-piece these 8 center-logs to the remainder of the blue strip of fabric to add the second log to each one, then press and cut them apart. Continue piecing in this manner to build eight 2-tier blocks (with 8 logs in each block) from the first strip of yellow fabric (A).

**NOTE:** If you want a slightly wonky effect for your center squares (as I did), vary your seam line slightly as you sew, making it a bit crooked. If you want the center squares to be neat and symmetrical, keep your seam line straight as usual.

4. Repeat steps 2 and 3 to build a second set of 8 blocks out from the remaining yellow strip of fabric (A).

## Assembling the Pillow Top

5. When you've completed all 16 blocks, press them neatly, and arrange them on the design board in 4 rows of 4 blocks each.

6. Using the column joining technique on page 32, join the first 4 blocks. Press. Join the second, third, and fourth columns of blocks.

7. Now join your first and second columns together, press, and repeat to join your second and third columns and third and fourth columns. Press the pillow top.

8. Using the adding borders technique on page 34, add 1"-wide border strips of fabric (B) to each side of the joined blocks to complete the pillow top, piecing if necessary. Press.

## Finishing the Pillow

9. Make a quilt sandwich with your backing, batting, and finished pillow top, and baste together, making sure that the layers are smooth and even. You are ready to quilt!

10. Using dark blue thread, begin to quilt using the stitch-in-the-ditch quilting method to stitch around the first tier of each block, framing the inner section of logs. Square up your pillow top.

11. Following the envelope pillow back technique on page 41, make a 2" double-fold hem (page 40) along one edge of each piece of pillow back fabric. Continue following the envelope pillow back technique to join the envelope closure to the pillow top, right sides together, using a ¼" seam allowance.

12. Clip the corners, if necessary. Turn the cover right side out, and press. Insert a 12" x 12" pillow form.

## Assembly Diagrams

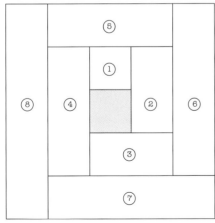

Block Assembly Diagram

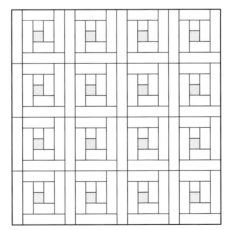

Front

Back

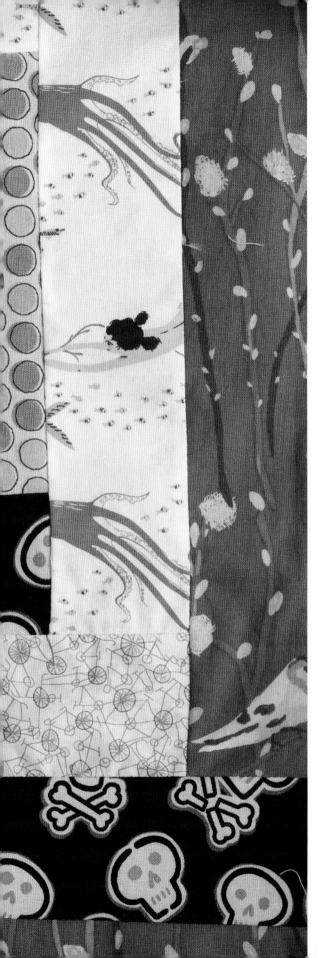

CHAPTER 5 BAGS+

 BEYOND

# DRAWSTRING **BAG**

**Difficulty:** 🧵

**Type of block:** Random

**Techniques used:** binding (page 39), button embellishment (page 40)

Make this simple bag from a single quilt block folded in half, lined with a lively contrast print, and edged with a binding-tape casing. I used a vintage quilt block for this bag and lined it with a cloth napkin, but I've made these bags with new blocks lined with yardage, too. I also added a little felt and crocheted-flower embellishment for fun.

**Finished center:** 3" x 3"

**Finished logs:** 1½" wide

**Finished block:** 15" x 15"

**Number of blocks:** 1

**Finished bag:** 15" x 7"

**You'll need:**

✽ One 16" x 16" quilt block

**NOTE:** I found the vintage quilt block at an estate sale, but you can also look for them at thrift stores or flea markets, or search Etsy and eBay. To make your own quilt block you'll need one 3½" x 3½" center square (A) and 16 assorted fabrics in 2"-wide strips, a total of ½ yard of fabric.

✽ Contrast fabric for lining, at least 16" x 16" (B)

✽ 1 yard 1"-wide binding tape

✽ 1½ yards ⅜"-wide grosgrain ribbon

✽ Small safety pin or elastic guide

✽ Thread (I used white to match my binding tape)

For optional embellishment:

✽ Remnant of green felt

✽ Small crocheted flower

✽ Fabric glue

✽ Hand-sewing needle and thread

✽ Button

| Cutting Key | A | B | Assorted |
|---|---|---|---|
| **Center Square** | | | |
| 3½" x 3½" | 1 | - | - |
| **Logs** | | | |
| 2" x 16" | - | - | 16 |
| **Lining** | | | |
| 16" x 16" | - | 1 | - |
| **To make your own 1" binding tape:** | | | |
| Cut a 36"-long strip of 2"-wide fabric. | | | |

## Cutting

1. Using the Cutting Key, cut and press the fabric needed for your bag. Follow the Block Assembly Diagram to create a 16" x 16" quilt block in the Random style using a colorful mix of patterns and colors.

## Assembling the Bag

2. Fold the quilt block in half, right sides together, and pin each of the 2 short ends together. Sew each end together securely with a ½" seam allowance, backstitching at the beginning and end to hold the seam.

   Repeat with the lining fabric. You will now have 2 sewn rectangles.

3. Turn the quilt block right side out and tuck the lining inside, wrong sides together, so that the unfinished edges match neatly.

4. Turn ¼" of the folded binding tape under and press it to create a neat edge. Pin the binding over both layers of fabric, beginning at one side seam, going all around the opening, and trim the other end ½" past the seam, turning it under and pressing it. This creates a casing for your drawstring.

5. Stitch the casing down all the way around the bag, leaving the pressed ends open. Using a safety pin or elastic guide, insert the ribbon into the casing and pull it all the way through so the ends extend out of each side of the casing.

6. Tie a knot at each end of the ribbon and trim the ends at an angle to keep them from fraying.

**Assembly Diagrams**

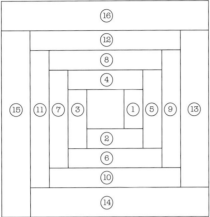

Block Assembly Diagram

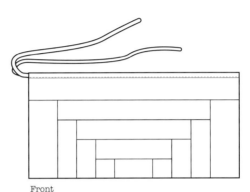

Front

## MAKING IT PERSONAL

My friend Linda Permann taught me how to crochet and patiently coached me stitch by stitch through my very first flower. I knew I wanted to save it for a special project, and this cute pouch was just the thing. Perhaps you have a special notion waiting for the right project as well! I made a felt "vine" dotted with leaves and the crocheted flower, finishing it with a button center. Here's how I made my embellishment:

**1.** To cut a 10" vine from green felt, just cut a simple, narrow rectangle with tapered ends. Also cut five 1"-long leaves, oval shapes ending in points.

**2.** Arrange the vine as you like (mine was near the top edge of the bag), with the leaves scattered along the length of the vine, and place the flower or other embellishment as desired. Stitch the flower and add a button as the center.

NOTE: To make a flower exactly like mine, check out Linda's book *Crochet Adorned* (Potter Craft, 2009).

**3.** Use fabric glue or hand-stitching to attach the vine and leaves. (You can also glue the felt down and then add a decorative running stitch with embroidery floss if you like!)

# EVERYTHING-IN-ONE-PLACE
# ZIP BAG

**Difficulty:** 🧵🧵🧵

**Type of block:** Random

**Techniques used:** spotlighting centers (page 28), row joining (page 32), diagonal quilting (page 35)

This handy zippered bag is perfect for carrying those small essentials like keys, wallet, phone, lip balm, and pen in a bigger handbag or tote. These go-to items are always quick to vanish to the deepest, darkest corners of my bag unless I corral them. But my favorite thing about this practical zip bag is that it's cute enough to carry solo like a clutch or stick it into a back pocket when traveling light.

To give the delicate fabrics some heft, I backed the bag's sides with denim—leftovers from the Market Tote (page 141)—and quilted over it just like batting. Use your favorite quilting-cotton scraps in any color combination that you like for this one!

**Finished center:** 1″ x 1″

**Finished logs:** 1″ wide

**Finished block:** 4½″ x 4½″

**Number of blocks:** 4

**Finished bag:** 9″ x 4½″

### You'll need:
* Scraps of 9 assorted colorful fabrics (see Cutting Key)
* Two 9½″ x 5″ pieces of denim for backing
* Two 9½″ x 5″ pieces of printed quilting cotton for lining (I used one of the same prints from the outside of the bag)
* 9″ zipper
* Zipper foot (optional)
* Thread (I used white)
* 1½″ x 1½″ piece of pattern paper

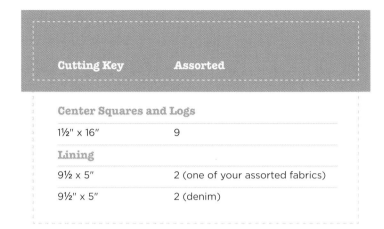

| Cutting Key | Assorted |
| --- | --- |
| **Center Squares and Logs** | |
| 1½" x 16" | 9 |
| **Lining** | |
| 9½ x 5" | 2 (one of your assorted fabrics) |
| 9½" x 5" | 2 (denim) |

## Cutting

1. Using the Block Assembly Diagram as a guide, swatch or hold together fabrics in 2 or 3 colors you want to use and play with the arrangements until you find a combination of fabrics you like. I used shades of brown and purple.

2. Using the Cutting Key, cut and press the fabric for the pouch. Use the pattern paper and the spotlighting centers technique to cut four 1½" x 1½" squares, either from the ends of 4 fabric strips, or from other parts of your scraps. I chose a horse, a button, an owl, and a floral design for my 4 center squares.

## Building the Blocks

3. Build the four 2-tier blocks beginning with log 1, choosing fabrics randomly. Use each fabric once in each block, varying each fabric's placement from block to block.

## Assembling the Bag

4. When you've completed all four blocks, press them neatly, and arrange them in 2 rows of 2

**Assembly Diagrams**

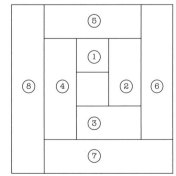

Block Assembly Diagram

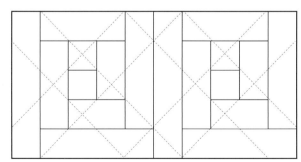

Front

blocks each, moving the blocks around to determine which 2 blocks you'd like to appear on each side of the pouch. I chose not to place like fabrics next to each other.

5. Using the two-way row joining technique on page 32, join each pair of blocks. Press both sides.

## Finishing the Bag

6. Now you'll mark your blocks for quilting. This pouch uses a two-direction diagonal quilting pattern (page 35). Using a quilting ruler and washable marker, mark diagonal lines along a 45-degree angle through the corners of the center squares as shown in the Quilting Diagram.

7. Place each finished pouch side on a piece of denim backing fabric, wrong sides together, and baste or pin them together, making sure the layers are smooth and even. You are ready to quilt!

8. Begin to quilt the crosshatch quilting lines from the bottom left corner of one side. Repeat to quilt the second side.

9. Pin one long edge of the zipper, zip head facing down, to the top edge of a pouch side, right sides facing. Use a zipper foot or ¼" piecing foot to sew. Backstitch at the beginning and end of your seam. In the same manner, pin and sew the second pouch side to the other side of the zipper. Open the zipper.

10. Pin the top edge of a piece of lining fabric to the zipper and the first side of the pouch, right sides together, catching one side of the opened zipper's edge between the 2 layers. Sew the lining to the zipper. In the same manner, pin and sew the second lining fabric to the other side of the pouch. Press both sides of the bag so that the outer side and lining surround the zipper neatly.

11. With the zipper open, pin and sew together the 3 nonzippered sides of the outer sections of the pouch, right sides together, using a ¼" seam allowance and catching the ends of the zipper inside the seams.

12. In the same manner, pin and sew together the 3 nonzippered sides of the lining, but leave 4" of the long side open for turning.

13. Turn the bag so the lining fits into the outer part of the pouch. Pin the opening closed and hand- or machine-stitch the opening closed. Place the lining inside the bag, and zip it up!

**Zipper Installation**

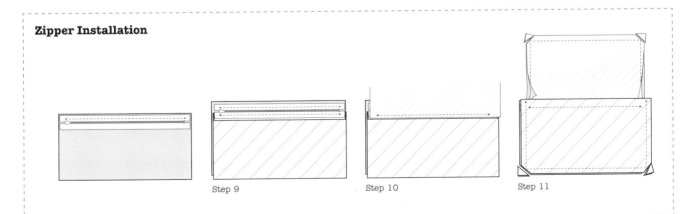

Step 9  Step 10  Step 11

# CHARMING **CAMERA CASE**

**Difficulty:** 🧵🧵🧵

**Type of block:** Color Story

**Techniques used:** spotlighting centers (page 28), row joining (page 32), stitch-in-the-ditch quilting (page 35), binding (page 38), button embellishment (page 40)

You can customize this simple case to fit your camera nicely. I found it best to make quilt blocks a few inches larger than needed, and then to trim them down evenly as I went—these blocks will work for a camera, phone or other gadget up to about 3" by 5". The finished case should be big enough for the camera to slip in easily but snug enough for it to stay in place.

**Finished center:** 2" x 2½"

**Finished logs:** 1" wide; 2" wide

**Finished block:** 6" x 7½"

**Number of blocks:** 2

**Binding:** about 12" (⅓ yard) of 2" binding, handmade or purchased

**Finished case:** 4" x 6"

**You'll need:**

✳ 2 fabric scraps, at least 2½" x 3", for center squares

✳ 8 fabric scraps (see Cutting Key)

✳ Two 12" x 7½" pieces of lining fabric, or sized to fit your camera case

✳ 2 pieces of quilt batting at least 6" x 7½" each, or sized to fit your camera case

✳ 12" of 2" (extra-wide) purchased binding, or 4" x 12" strip of fabric for binding and 2" binding-tape maker, if making your own

✳ 2 small squares of sew-in Velcro

✳ 2 medium or large buttons (mine were about 1" across)

✳ Any embellishments you choose

✳ Thread (I used white)

✳ 2½" x 3" piece of pattern paper

| Cutting Key | Assorted | |
| --- | --- | --- |
| **Center Squares** | | |
| 2½" x 3" | 2 | |
| **Logs** | | |
| 1½" x 6" (2 and 4) | 4 | |
| 2½" x 6" (1 and 3) | 4 | |
| **Lining (sized to fit your camera)** | | |
| 12" x 7½" | 1 | |
| **If making your own 2" binding:** | | |
| Cut a 12" strip of 4"-wide fabric (solid color). | | |

## Cutting

1. Using the Block Assembly Diagram as a guide, swatch or hold together fabrics in colors you want to use and play with the arrangements until you find a combination of 8 to 10 fabrics you like. I chose bright, cheerful prints in blue, orange, white, and green left over from birthday pennants I made for my daughter.

2. Using the Cutting Key, cut the fabric for the camera case. Use the pattern paper and the spot-lighting centers technique to cut the 2 center squares.

## Building the Blocks

3. Build a one-tier block according to the Block Assembly Diagram, beginning with log 1. Piece the wide logs along the short sides of the center rectangle and the narrow logs to the long sides of the center rectangle. Repeat to build a second block. Press the blocks neatly.

## Assembling the Case

4. Using the two-way row joining technique on page 32, join the blocks together along one long edge to create a rectangular patchwork piece, backstitching at the beginning and end to hold the seam. Press. Add embroidery or other embellishment to the patchwork, if desired.

5. Stack 2 pieces of quilt batting just slightly larger than your joined blocks. Stack the batting pieces together, pin them to the wrong side of the patchwork piece, and stitch all 3 layers together along the seam that joins the blocks. (The double layer of batting will give more protection to your camera.) Square up the blocks, trimming away the excess batting. You are ready to quilt!

6. Begin to quilt using stitch-in-the-ditch quilting around the center squares only. Trim away the excess batting.

**NOTE:** Stitch-in-the-ditch quilting lines add stability to the camera case and will make the center squares "pop" against the smooth, nonquilted background.

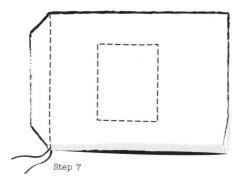

Step 7

**7.** Fold the quilted piece, right sides together, along the stitched seam. Stitch along one short edge using a ½" seam allowance and trim the corners as shown. This outer case will look like a fleecy sleeping bag.

**8.** Slip your camera into the outer case and mark where the seam should fall along the long open end; the camera should fit snugly but not tightly. Sew along this line and then test how your camera fits into the finished sleeve. Redo this seam if it's not quite right. When you're pleased with the fit, trim the excess batting and turn the case right side out.

**9.** Fold the lining fabric, right sides together, and stitch it into a "sleeping bag" the same size as the outer case layers as you did in steps 6 and 7.

**10.** Put the lining into the case, using your camera (or a chopstick if easier) to slide it all the way in. Now check to see how far in your camera sits; trim the open edge of all layers if they extend more than 1" to 1½" beyond the camera.

**11.** Measure your camera-case opening all the way around, and add ½". Cut a piece of binding tape to this length. Using a ¼" seam allowance, stitch the unfinished ends of your binding tape together, right sides together, and press the edges down. Fold the binding over the unfinished edges of the camera case opening to bind the lining and the outer case together. Pin and sew on the binding. Backstitch at the beginning and end of the stitching to hold it in place.

**12.** Pin and machine-stitch the Velcro pieces in place, centered on each side of the inside lining. Using the button embellishment technique on page 40, hand-sew a decorative button on the outer case to hide the Velcro stitching. I chose to use 2 different colors of the same style vintage button to complement the 2 sides of the case. Add any other decorative flourishes you like! I sewed on 1 tiny button as an "eye" for the rhino printed on one of my center squares, just for fun.

### Assembly Diagrams

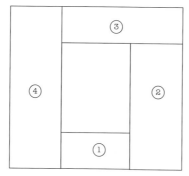

Block Assembly Diagram

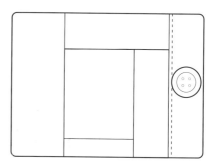

Front

# MARKET TOTE

**Difficulty:** 🧵🧵🧵

**Type of block:** Picture Frame

**Techniques used:** double-fold hem (page 40), patch pocket (page 41), topstitching (page 52)

This sturdy, eye-catching market bag gives new life to a couple of pairs of old jeans. I combined dark and light denim for maximum contrast, but a more subtle color mix would be nice, too. Line it with a lively print or a calm solid and add a patch pocket inside for your keys, wallet, and shopping list.

**Finished center:** 4″ x 4″

**Finished logs:** 1½″ wide

**Finished block:** 16″ x 16″

**Number of blocks:** 2

**Finished tote:** 16″ x 16″ x 6″, with 30″ handles

**NOTE:** Piece these blocks clockwise since the seams of the heavy fabric will press outward more easily. Remember to piece with a slightly larger seam allowance, ³⁄₈″ instead of the usual ¼″.

## You'll need:

* 1 pair of dark denim jeans, or ½ yard of dark denim fabric (A)
* 1 pair of light denim jeans, or ⅔ yard of light denim fabric (B)
* 1 pair of denim jeans, any color wash (if needed), or use included yardage of denim fabric (A and B)
* ⅔ yard lining fabric (C)
* Thread (I used blue)
* Loop turner

| Cutting Key | A | B | C |
|---|---|---|---|

**NOTE:** Cut your dark-denim center squares and light-denim panels first, and then cut the long strips for logs and handles (lengthwise and on grain). When cutting fabrics into strips, your length will depend on the size and shape of the reclaimed garment. Scrap-piece strips together to get the length you need for each log. If you need to mix and match different denims to achieve the yardage needed, keep in mind that the wrong side of the dark fabrics may be closer in color. This project uses 100" total of 2" strips of fabric (A) and 200" total of 2" strips of fabric (B). The any-denim panels for the bottom of the bag can be cut last if need be.

| Center Squares | A | B | C |
|---|---|---|---|
| 4½" x 4½" | 2 | - | - |

| Tote Panels | A | B | C |
|---|---|---|---|
| 6½" x 16" | - | 2 for sides | - |
| 6½" x 16" — 2 any denim for reinforced bottom | | | |

| Logs and Tote Handles | A | B | C |
|---|---|---|---|
| 2" x 100" (in pieces of any length) | 1 | - | - |
| 2" x 200" (in pieces of any length) | - | 1 | - |

**NOTE:** You'll use four 31" lengths of light denim for tote handles, included in this total measurement.

| Lining | A | B | C |
|---|---|---|---|
| 16" x 16" | - | - | 2 |
| 6½" x 16" | - | - | 3 |
| 8" x 6½" (pocket) | - | - | 1 |

## Cutting

1. Prepare the jeans for cutting by removing the waistband, side seams, and hems. You will have 4 long sections of fabric (the front and back of each leg). Using the Cutting Key, cut and press the fabric for the tote. Set the center squares aside and cut all log strips lengthwise, along the straight grain, for logs.

## Building the Blocks

2. Build a 4-tier block according to the Block Assembly Diagram. Beginning with log 1, piece the first tier, then alternate the fabrics with each subsequent tier, (B), (A), (B), (A), for a concentric squares effect. Press the block neatly. Repeat to piece a second block. You have now made the front and back sides of the bag.

## Making the Tote Handles

**3.** Pin and sew 2 of the 31″ light denim strips, right sides together, along both long sides using a scant ¼″ seam allowance. Repeat to join the remaining 31″-long strips to each other. Use a loop turner to turn both handles right sides out.

**4.** Press, and topstitch the handles ⅛″ from the long edges. Set aside.

## Making the Tote Bottom and Sides

**5.** Place two 6½″ x 16″ fabric panels (of any denim color) together and stitch a wide zigzag pattern back and forth across the width of the panels to securely quilt them together. These reinforced panels will become the bottom of your tote.

**6.** With right sides together, align and sew together the short ends of one 6½″ x 16″ light denim side panel and the reinforced bottom panel. In the same manner, sew the remaining 6½″ x 16″ light denim panel to the other side of the bottom panel. These strips are now the sides of your tote.

**7.** Repeat step 6 to join the three 16″ x 6½″ lining pieces end to end, right sides together.

**8.** Using the patch pocket technique on page 41, make a patch pocket using the 8″ piece of lining fabric (C). The ½″ double-fold hem should be made on an 8″ edge.

**9.** Pin the pocket on the right side of one 16″ piece of lining fabric, centered side to side and about 2½″ from the top edge. Stitch your pocket in place, using the pocket corners technique to reinforce the stitching.

### Assembly Diagrams

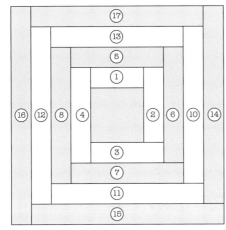

Block Assembly Diagram

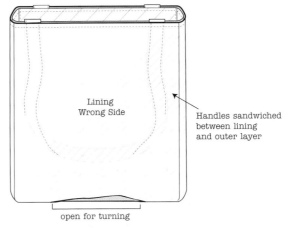

Lining Wrong Side

Handles sandwiched between lining and outer layer

open for turning

Bag Assembly

10. Pin the 3-part lining to the piece of lining fabric with the pocket, right sides together, matching the corners of the pocket piece with the seams of the 3-part lining. The pocket should open away from the bottom of the tote. Sew together. Pin and sew the other long edge of the lining section to the remaining piece of lining fabric the same way, but leave an 8″ opening on one edge for turning.

11. Repeat step 10 to sew your first denim block to the tote bottom and sides, right sides together. In the same manner, join the remaining block (without leaving an opening).

## Finishing the Tote

12. Pin a handle strip to the front of the bag, matching the unfinished edges with the top edge of the bag, and aligning the handles with the third tier of logs. Sew the handles to the bag at both ends, ¼″ from the top edge of the tote, stitching twice to secure.

    Repeat to sew the remaining handle strip to the back of the bag.

13. Turn the tote right side out, with handles hanging down to the front and back. Turn the lining wrong side out and place the tote inside it, with the handles sandwiched in between the 2 layers. Pin and stitch around the perimeter of the tote's opening, ¼″ from the unfinished edge.

14. Turn your tote right side out through the opening in the lining. Press, pin, and stitch the lining opening closed.

15. Press, pin, and topstitch the outside of the tote and the lining around the opening.

16. Pin and topstitch along all of the perimeter seams on the outside of the tote to reinforce them.

# FAVORITE FABRICS **BAG**

**Difficulty:** 🧵🧵🧵🧵

**Type of blocks:** Random/Sunshine and Shadow

**Techniques used:** spotlighting centers (page 28), binding (to construct handles) (page 38), double-fold hem (page 40), patch pocket (page 41)

DESIGNED BY DANIELA CAINE

This roomy bag is the perfect place to use up and memorialize some of your favorite fabrics that are just too precious to go to waste. Each block is based on the traditional Sunshine and Shadow log cabin style. The new twist in the design? Instead of clustering light and dark values together, you'll create a dynamic visual effect by alternating values (and favorite fabrics) across each block.

**Finished center:** 4" x 4"

**Finished logs:** 2"

**Finished block:** 19½" x 25"

**Number of blocks:** 2

**Finished bag:** 19" x 25"

**NOTE:** If you are using lightweight fabrics in conjunction with sturdier ones, fuse interfacing to the lightweight logs, or fuse interfacing to the entire finished blocks before you line the bag. You will need two 19½" x 25" pieces of additional interfacing to do so.

## You'll need:

❋ ¾ yard main fabric (A)

❋ ½ yard coordinating fabric (B)

❋ 1 fat quarter fabric (C)

❋ 1 fat quarter fabric (D)

❋ 1 fat quarter fabric (E)

❋ Two 4" x 4" pieces of fabric for center squares (F)

❋ ¼ yard light- to medium-weight interfacing (for handles)

❋ ¾ yard lining fabric (G)

❋ 7" zipper

❋ Zipper foot (optional)

❋ 4" x 4" piece of pattern paper

| Cutting Key | A | Assorted |
|---|---|---|
| **Center Squares** | | |
| 4" x 4" | - | 2 (F) |
| **Logs** | | |
| 2" x 220" | - | 1 (A) |
| 2" x 178" | - | 1 (B) |
| 2" x 116" | - | 1 (C) |
| 2" x 40" | - | 1 (D) |
| 2" x 22" | - | 1 (E) |
| **Handles** | | |
| 4" x 29" | 2 | - |
| **Lining** | | |
| 7½" x 6½" (pocket) | 1 | - |
| 9" x 7" (pocket) | 1 | - |
| 25" x 19½" (Lining) | - | 2 |
| **Interfacing** | | |
| 4" x 29" | - | 2 |

## Cutting

1. Using the Block Assembly Diagram as a guide, swatch or hold together fabrics you love for the center and logs of this bag, making sure that there is a mix of light and dark values. I used prints in pinks, blacks, and whites for lovely contrast within my blocks, and I decided on a black print for my handles and pocket details. I lined the bag with solid black cotton.

2. Using the Cutting Key, cut and press the fabric for your bag. Use the pattern paper and the spotlighting centers technique to cut the center squares.

## Building the Blocks

3. Build the first block clockwise according to the Block Assembly Diagram, beginning with fabric (E) as the first, shortest log above the center square. You'll use light-colored fabric for logs 1 and 2 and dark-colored fabric for logs 3 and 4. Piece and press the seam allowances away from the center.

   Continue adding tiers according the Block Assembly Diagram. Each tier "mirrors" the light and dark values of the previous, so you will use dark-colored fabric for logs 5 and 6, light-colored fabric for logs 7 and 8, and so on until you've completed 5 tiers.

## Assembly Diagrams

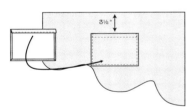

Block Assembly Diagram

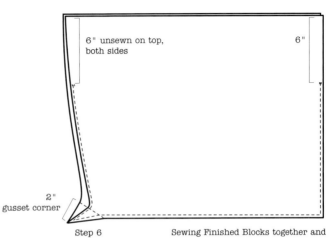

6" unsewn on top, both sides

6"

2" gusset corner

Step 6

Sewing Finished Blocks together and creating a gusset corner

3½"

Lining: Patch Pocket
Step 7

3½"

3½"

Lining: Zipper Pocket
Step 8

Handle preparation
Step 13

Favorite Fabrics Bag Handle Installation
Step 15

4. Piece 2 additional strips to both sides to create a rectangular shape, as shown in the Block Assembly Diagram (page 147), alternating the color values. Press.

5. Repeat steps 3 and 4 to build a second block.

### Assembling the Bag

6. Position finished blocks right sides together, and leaving the upper edge open, sew around 3 sides, starting and ending with a back stitch 6" from the upper edge. The fourth side stays unsewn. Before turning the bag right side out, sew gusset corners 2" deep to create the bag's base.

7. Using the patch pocket technique on page 41, make a patch pocket using the 7½" piece of fabric (A). The ¼" double-fold hem (page 40) should be made on a 7½" edge. Pin the pocket on the right side of a 25" lining piece, centered side to side and about 3½" from the top edge. Stitch your pocket in place, using the pocket corners technique to reinforce the stitching.

8. Make a zipper pocket. Align the closed zipper, zip head down, flush along the long top edge of the 9" piece of fabric (A), right sides facing. Leave a 1" seam allowance on each end of the zipper. Fold in the ends of the zipper tape so they can be caught in the line of stitching. Pin in place. Using a zipper foot, stitch the zipper tape down, starting and ending with a backstitch. Fold the remaining 3 sides of the pocket ¼" to the wrong side, and press.

9. Mark the zipper placement on the remaining 25" lining piece, centered side to side and about 3½" from the top edge. Place the zipper pocket wrong side up so that the unsewn zipper tape

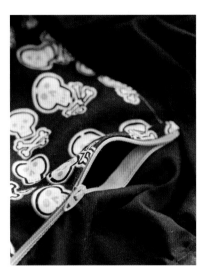

aligns with the marking, zip head down. Fold in the seam allowances of the zipper tape ends again, pin, and stitch into place. Backstitch at the beginning and end of the stitching. Fold the zipper pocket down, so the right side is facing up. Pin and stitch the pocket in place along the 3 open sides.

10. Sew the 2 lining pieces, right sides together, starting and ending 6" from the upper edges, and leaving a 6"-long opening at the bottom of the lining for turning. Shape the corners in the same manner as you did for the outer bag in step 6. Don't turn the bag yet!

11. Place the outer bag into the lining bag, right sides together. Pin and stitch together the open edges of the 6"-long unsewn sections at the top of the outer bag and lining on both sides. Turn the bag so the outer bag is right side out. Stitch the opening at the bottom of the lining closed.

12. Pin the outer bag and lining together at the top edge. Sew 2 rows of long basting stitches along the upper edge, catching both faric layers, and gather to 11" length. Repeat with the second side. Set aside.

## Making the Handles

13. Iron the interfacing to the wrong side of the handle strips, following the manufacturer's directions. Fold and press the strips in half lengthwise, wrong sides together, and then 1" to the wrong side along both side edges so the edges meet at the center crease line. Press.

14. Fold each handle strip in half lengthwise, right sides together, and stitch the loose ends together to make a loop. Press seam allowances open.

## Attaching the Handles

15. With the insides of the bag facing, align the open edge of the handle loop over the gathered edge of the bag. Fold the handle strap over the gathered seam allowance along the pressed folds and pin in place. Topstitch the handle strip closed, stitching through all layers all around. Repeat to attach the remaining handle strip to the opposite side of the bag.

# RED CROSS **BAG**

**Difficulty:** 🧵🧵🧵

**Type of block:** Sunshine and Shadow (variation)

**Techniques used:** chain-piecing (page 31), row joining (page 32), stitch-in-the-ditch quilting (page 35), binding (page 38), button embellishment (page 40), patch pocket (page 41)

This bag design is an updated twist on the traditional Sunshine and Shadow style, which pairs light and dark logs around a small center square. The trick here is that this whole design is made with one fabric, a brick-red corduroy: The textured (right) side makes up the dark sections, while the flat (wrong) side of the fabric provides the contrasting lighter sections. In addition, I modified the design by using my "dark" strips for an outer rim of bold color and texture, making a slightly off-kilter quilt block. When the four blocks are joined at the dark-log edges, a simple, striking cross design pops from the center.

**Finished centers:** 1″ x 1″

**Finished logs:** 1″ wide

**Finished block:** 7½″ x 7½″

**Number of blocks:** 8

**Binding:** about 68″ (2 yards) of ¾″ binding, hand-made or purchased

**Finished bag:** 16″ x 16″

**You'll need:**

* 1 yard brick-red corduroy (or the color of your choice; make sure the front and back of the fabric have good contrast) (A)
* ¾ yard medium-weight denim for backing (B)
* ¾ yard quilting cotton for lining and binding (C)
* Thread to match the lining and corduroy
* 1¼″ covered button kit
* 4″ length of very thin elastic (I used a hair band)
* ¾″ binding-tape maker (recommended)

| Cutting Key | A | B | C |
|---|---|---|---|

**NOTE:** You may need to join strips of fabric to achieve the 42″ lengths necessary for the bag sides, lining, and backing.

| Cutting Key | A | B | C |
|---|---|---|---|
| **Center Square** | | | |
| 1½″ x 1½″ | 8 | - | - |
| **Logs** | | | |
| 1½″ x 36″ | 14 | - | - |
| **Bag Handles** | | | |
| 1½″ x 34″ | 2 | - | - |
| **Bag Sides** | | | |
| 2¼″ x 42″ | 1 | - | - |
| **Lining** | | | |
| 2¼″ x 42″ | - | - | 1 |
| 8″ x 6″ | - | - | 1 |

**NOTE:** You'll also need a 16″ x 32″ piece of uncut lining fabric for step 8, so consider this when cutting the lining pieces listed above in the Cutting Key.

| Cutting Key | A | B | C |
|---|---|---|---|
| **Backing** | | | |
| 1½″ x 34″ | - | 1 | - |
| 2¼″ x 42″ | - | 1 | - |

**NOTE:** You'll also need at least a 16″ x 32″ piece of uncut backing fabric for step 8, so consider this when cutting the backing pieces listed above in the Cutting Key.

**To make your own ¾″ finished binding:**

Cut two 34″-long, 1½″-wide strips of fabric (C).

## Cutting

1. Using the Cutting Key, cut the fabric for the bag. Cut your corduroy logs and handles lengthwise, with the grain, so the striped texture/wales run the length of the logs—even if this mean cutting parallel to the selvages instead of perpendicular, as you normally do for log cabin logs. Do not cut the lining fabric yet.

## Building the Blocks

2. *Using the flat (wrong) side of the corduroy as the right side*, chain-piece 4 center squares to a strip of fabric. This fabric will become the first log in these blocks. Trim the logs and press the front and back of the blocks with the seams away form the centers. Trim and press the back and front of the blocks with the seams away from the centers.

Working clockwise, continue chain-piecing and pressing the second tier of logs.

3. Chain-piece the first half of a third tier of logs (9 and 10), *using the textured side of the corduroy as the right side*, as shown in the Block Assembly Diagram. Press. Then chain-piece an additional half tier of logs to logs 9 and 10. Press.

4. Repeat steps 2 and 3 to construct a total of 8 identical blocks.

## Assembling the Blocks

5. When you've completed all 8 blocks, press them neatly. Arrange them as shown on the Assembly Diagram, positioning blocks in groups of 4 with the dark, textured logs meeting in the middle to achieve a cross design. You will have 2 groups of 4 blocks each.

6. Using the four-way row joining technique on page 32, join each group of 4 blocks to form the front and the back of your bag.

## Making the Tote Bottom and Sides

7. Measure in 1″ diagonally from the bottom corners on the front and back bag pieces and mark a curved line, as shown on the Assembly Diagram. Cut along the curve to make each piece into a U shape.

8. Use the bag front as a template, and place it on the uncut lining fabric. Cut 2 U shapes the same size. In the same manner, cut 2 U shapes from the denim backing fabric.

9. Pin the first U-shaped denim backing piece to the bag front, wrong sides together, and stitch in the ditch along each seam between the flat and textured fabrics to emphasize and outline the cross design. Repeat with the remaining denim backing piece and the bag back.

10. Press, pin, and edgestitch the denim and bag pieces together along the perimeter of the U shape.

11. Edgestitch the long sides of the 42″ strips of corduroy and denim backing fabric, wrong sides facing. This continuous panel forms the sides and bottom of your bag.

12. Pin this long panel piece to the perimeter of the bag front, right sides together. Make small gathers or pleats in the bag front where necessary around the curved corners. Stitch using a ⅜″ seam allowance. In the same manner, sew the unfinished long side of the long panel to the bag back.

13. Using the pocket corners technique on page 41, make a patch pocket using the 8″ piece of lining fabric. The ½″ double-fold hem should be made on an 8″ edge. Pin the pocket on the right side of a U-shaped lining piece, centered side to side and about 3½″ from the top edge. Stitch your pocket in place, using the pocket corners technique to reinforce the stitching.

14. Repeat step 12 to pin and stitch your long lining panel to the front and back lining.

### Making the Bag Handles

**15.** Place a 34″ strip of corduroy, textured side down, on your work surface and stack a 34″ strip of denim backing fabric and the remaining 34″ strip of corduroy, textured side up, on top. Edge-stitch or pin together the layers.

**16.** Pin one 34″ length of the binding to each long side of the strap and bind.

### Assembling the Bag

**17.** Now you're ready to assemble your bag! Turn the bag right side out and the lining wrong side out. Press the unfinished edges ³⁄₈″ to the wrong side of the bag body and to the wrong side of the lining. Put the lining inside the bag, matching the seams and tucking the unfinished edges inside, and pin in place.

**18.** Place one end of the strap inside 1 narrow side of the bag, sandwiching it between the body and lining, and pin in place. Do the same with the opposite end of the strap on the opposite side of the bag. Finally, shape the 4″ length of elastic into a loop. At the center back of the bag, tuck the unfinished edges of the elastic between the lining and the bag. Pin in place.

**19.** Stitch around the perimeter of the bag's opening, catching the loop and both straps securely while joining the lining and the bag body. Backstitch at the beginning and end to secure the line of stitching.

**20.** Make a 1¼″ covered button using a scrap of the lining fabric and your button kit, following the manufacturer's instructions. Sew it to the front of your bag, centered ¾″ from the top edge. Loop the elastic around the button to hold the bag closed.

**Assembly Diagrams**

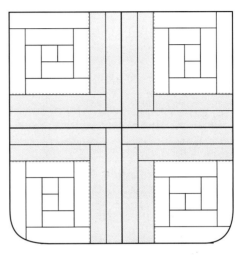

Block Assembly Diagram

4-Block Assembly Diagram

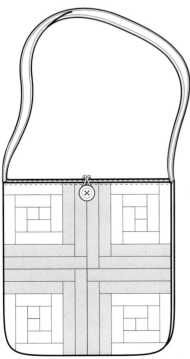

Front

Handle/Lining Assembly

# RESOURCES

These are some of my favorite quilting books for reference and inspiration—both for learning inspiring quilting techniques and methods, and to find out more about fascinating quilt history and culture.

## BOOKS

### ✳ Quilting techniques ✳

*Denyse Schmidt Quilts: 30 Colorful Quilt and Patchwork Projects* by Denyse Schmidt (Chronicle Books, 2005).

*I Love Patchwork: 21 Irresistible Zakka Projects to Sew* by Rashida Coleman-Hale (Interweave Press, 2009).

*Log Cabin ABCs,* by Marti Michell (Marti Michell, 2008).

*Log Cabin Quilts Unlimited: The Ultimate Creative Guide to the Most Popular and Versatile Pattern* by Patricia Cox and Maggi McCormick Gordon (Creative Publishing International, 2004).

*Material Obsession: Modern Quilts with Traditional Roots* by Kathy Doughty and Sarah Fielke (STC Craft, 2009).

*The Modern Quilt Workshop: Patterns, Techniques, and Designs from the FunQuilts Studio* by Weeks Ringle and Bill Kerr (Quarry Books, 2005).

*Patchwork Style: 35 Simple Projects for a Cozy & Colorful Life* by Suzuko Koseki (Trumpeter, 2009).

*The Practical Guide to Patchwork: New Basics for the Modern Quiltmaker* by Elizabeth Hartman (C&T, 2010).

*The Quilter's Ultimate Visual Guide: From A to Z—Hundreds of Tips and Techniques for Successful Quiltmaking* by Ellen Pahl (Rodale Press, 1997).

*Quilting for Peace: Make the World a Better Place One Stitch at a Time* by Katherine Bell (STC Craft, 2009).

### ✳ Quilting history and culture ✳

*Abstract Design in American Quilts: A Biography of an Exhibition* by Jonathan Holstein (Kentucky Quilt Project, 2001).

*America's Quilts and Coverlets* by Carleton L. Safford and Robert Bishop (Bonanza Books, 1985).

*Quilts of the Oregon Trail* by Mary Bywater Cross (Schiffer Publishing, 2007).

*American Quilts in the Modern Age, 1870–1940: The International Quilt Study Center Collections* by Marin F. Hanson and Patricia Cox Crews, eds. (University of Nebraska Press, 2009).

*Gee's Bend: The Architecture of the Quilt* by Paul Arnett et al (Tinwood Books, 2006).

*Ho for California!: Pioneer Women and Their Quilts* by Jean Ray Laury and California Heritage Quilt Project (Dutton, 1990).

*The Pieced Quilt: An American Design Tradition* by Jonathan Holstein (New York Graphic Society, 1973).

*The Quilts of Gee's Bend: Masterpieces from a Lost Place* by John Beardsley and others (Tinwood Books in Association with the Museum of Fine Arts, Houston, 2002).

### ✳ Embellishments and extras ✳

I also love and highly recommend each of these general craft books, which are invaluable for adding all kinds of embellishments and details to quilt projects.

*Appliqué Your Way: 35 Pretty Sewing Projects and Patterns* by Kayte Terry (Chronicle, 2009).

*Bend the Rules with Fabric: Sewing Projects with Stencils, Stamps, Dye, Photo Transfers, Silk Screening, and More* by Amy Karol (Potter Craft, 2009).

*Button It Up: 80 Amazing Vintage Button Projects for Necklaces, Bracelets, Embellishments, House-wares and More* by Susan Beal (Taunton Press, 2009).

*Color Your Cloth: A Quilter's Guide to Dyeing and Patterning Fabric* by Malka Dubrawsky (Lark Books, 2009).

*Crochet Adorned: Reinvent Your Wardrobe with Crocheted Accents, Embellishments, and Trims* by Linda Permann (Potter Craft, 2009).

*Embroidered Effects: Projects and Patterns to Inspire Your Stitching* (Chronicle Books, 2009) and *Sublime Stitching: Hundreds of Hip Embroidery Patterns and How-To* by Jenny Hart (Chronicle Books, 2006).

*Embroidery Companion: Classic Designs for Modern Living* (Potter Craft, 2010) and *Stitched in Time: Memory-Keeping Projects to Sew and Share from the Creator of Posie Gets Cozy* by Alicia Paulson (Potter Craft, 2008).

## GENERAL RESOURCES

**Fabric Shoppers Unite,** fabricshoppersunite.com

Shop local! Find your closest independent quilting and fabric shops using the handy geographic search tools on this website.

**The International Quilt Study Center,** explorer.quiltstudy.org

The largest public collection of quilts in the world, archived online, with many amazing extras to explore.

**The Modern Quilt Guild,** themodernquiltguild.com

A lively and fantastic guild for modern quilters, with U.S. and international chapters—find and join your local guild or start a new one for your area.

**True Up,** trueup.net
True Up covers all things fabric, sewing, and quilting, including weekly U.S. and international sale announcements.

### ❋ Shops ❋

**Bolt Fabric Boutique,** boltfabricboutique.com
2136 NE Alberta St.
Portland, Oregon 97211
(503) 287-2658

A very modern collection of vivid prints, imported fabrics, and other ultra-tempting fabric, patterns, and notions.

**Cool Cottons,** coolcottons.biz
2417 Southeast Hawthorne Blvd.
Portland, Oregon 97214
(503) 232-0417
My neighborhood fabric shop, beautifully organized by color. Every direction you turn brings more inspiration.

**Etsy.com**
Many Etsy shops carry remarkable new, vintage, and imported fabric and notions. Search by keyword and bookmark your favorite shops.

**Exclusive Buttons**
10252 San Pablo Ave.
El Cerrito, CA 94530
(510) 524-5606
You have to see this amazing shop to believe it— it's filled with vintage buttons from floor to ceiling. I've found some of my favorite treasures here.

**FabricWorm,** fabricworm.com
Fresh, modern quilting cottons and Japanese fabrics.

**Fat Quarter Shop,** fatquartershop.com
A huge shop specializing in, yes, fat quarters, along with other specialty cuts.

**Pendleton Woolen Mill Store,** thewoolenmillstore.blogspot.com
8500 Southeast McLoughlin Blvd.
Portland, OR 97222
(503) 535-5786
Buy from the Pendleton Woolen Mill Store on eBay, or call the store directly. This is a wonderful source for Pendleton yardage and notions—an amazing resource.

**Pink Chalk Fabrics,** pinkchalkfabrics.com
A lovely mix of fabric, kits, notions, and more.

**Purl Soho,** purlsoho.com
459 Broome St.
New York, NY 10013
(212) 420-8796
A gorgeously inviting New York City store carrying fabrics, wool felt, notions and many other treasures, with a charming online shop and blog.

# ✳ ACKNOWLEDGMENTS ✳

First, thank you so much to my editors: Betty Wong, who shaped my first ideas into this beautiful book, and Rebecca Behan, whose skillful edits sharpened every page. Thanks to my always-stellar agent, Stacey Glick, for her expert guidance, and to Kevin Kosbab for his knowledgeable copyedits. Thank you to Alexis Hartman for the lovely illustrations, and to Alexandra Grablewski, Marcus Tullis, and Heather Weston for the luminous photographs.

I especially want to thank Daniela Caine, who not only contributed two gorgeous projects of her own (the Northwest Modern Quilt and the Favorite Fabrics Handbag), but created the wonderfully clear assembly diagrams for each project, and even helped me polish off the legions of Modern Crosses and Market Totes at a super-fun dining-room-table quilting bee. Thank you to Sue Kopp for sharing your vast quilting experience through your fantastic technical editing. And thank you to Lea Keohane for cheerfully cutting several massive quilts' worth of fabric!

Thank you so much to the Aurora Colony Historical Society, the Benton County Historical Society, Elizabeth Hartman, and Alissa Haight Carlton for generously sharing their lovely log cabin quilt photographs, antique and modern, for this book.

Another round of thank-yous go to Sarah Schlosser Moon, Joshua Moon, Andy Caine, Kim Kight, Caitlin Devereaux, Linda Permann, Natalie Zee Drieu, and my dear crafty friends near and far for your enthusiasm and feedback. Thank you to Pam and Marie at Cool Cottons, Gina and Amy at Bolt, Kathy at Pendleton Wool, and Sarah at Powell's Books, and the Modern Quilt Guild for generous help and inspiration. And thank you to Denyse Schmidt for the dazzling weekend of improvisational patchwork that started the year of this book off so beautifully.

Finally, a heartfelt thank-you to my husband, Andrew, for his unwavering support, encouragement, and love as every room of our house filled with fabric and batting. I am so lucky to have you as my partner in life and in craft. Thank you to our daughter Pearl for her love of buttons and for all the kisses when I was finally done for the day, and a special thank-you to our baby son for inspiring just the right design for the tenth quilt before we even met.

# ✳ INDEX ✳